from G
Som

GW01457869

?.

the lives and times of archy and mehitabel

books by
don marquis

don marquis

the lives and times of archy & mehitabel

with pictures by george herriman
and an introduction by e. b. white

doubleday & company, inc.
garden city, new york

copyright, 1927, 1930, 1933, 1935, 1950
by doubleday and company, inc.
copyright, 1916, 1917, 1918, 1919, 1920, 1921, 1922
by sun printing and publishing association.
copyright, 1922, 1923, 1924, 1925, 1934
by new york tribune, inc.
copyright, 1925, 1926, 1933, 1934
by p. f. collier and son, company.
copyright, 1928, 1932, 1933
by don marquis.
all rights reserved.

isbn: 0-385-04262-0
printed in the united states

dedicated to babs
    with babs knows what
    and babs knows why

acknowledgment

the author is indebted to the proprietors of the new york sun, the new york herald-tribune, new york herald-tribune magazine and p. f. collier and son company for permission to reprint these sketches.

contents

archy and mehitabel

[ix]

archy s life of mehitabel

[xi]

archy does his part

introduction

When the publisher asked me to write a few introductory remarks about Don Marquis for this new edition of *archy and mehitabel,* he said in his letter: "The sales of this particular volume have been really astounding."

They do not astound me. Among books of humor by American authors, there are only a handful that rest solidly on the shelf. This book about Archy and Mehitabel, hammered out at such awful cost by the bug hurling himself at the keys, is one of those books. It is funny, it is wise, it is tender, and it is tough. The sales do not astound me; only the author astounds me, for I know (or think I do) at what cost Don Marquis produced these gaudy and irreverent tales. He was the sort of poet who does not create easily; he was left unsatisfied and gloomy by what he produced; day and night he felt the juices squeezed out of him by the merciless demands of daily newspaper work; he was never quite certified by intellectuals and serious critics of belles lettres. He ended in an exhausted condition—his money gone, his strength gone. Describing the coming of Archy in the Sun Dial column of the New York *Sun* one afternoon in 1916, he wrote: "After about an hour of this frightfully difficult literary labor he fell to the floor exhausted, and we saw him creep feebly into a nest of the poems which are always there in profusion." In that sentence Don Marquis was writing his own obituary notice. After about a lifetime of frightfully difficult literary labor keeping newspapers supplied with copy, he fell exhausted.

I feel obliged, before going any further, to dispose of one troublesome matter. The reader will have perhaps noticed that I am capitalizing the name Archy and the name Mehitabel. I mention this because the capitalization of Archy is considered the unforgivable sin by a whole raft of old Sun Dial fans who have somehow nursed the illogical idea that because Don Marquis's cockroach was incapable of operating the shift key of a typewriter, nobody else could operate it. This is preposterous. Archy himself wished to be capitalized—he was no e. e. cummings. In fact he once flirted with the idea of writing the story of his life all in capital letters, if he could get somebody to lock the shift key for him. Furthermore, I capitalize Archy on the highest authority: wherever in his columns Don Marquis referred to his hero, Archy was capitalized by the boss himself. What higher authority can you ask?

The device of having a cockroach leave messages in his typewriter in the *Sun* office was a lucky accident and a happy solution for an acute problem. Marquis did not have the patience to adjust himself easily and comfortably to the rigors of daily columning, and he did not go about it in the steady, conscientious way that (for example) his contemporary Franklin P. Adams did. Consequently Marquis was always hard up for stuff to fill his space. Adams was a great editor, an insatiable proofreader, a good make-up man. Marquis was none of these. Adams, operating his Conning Tower in the *World,* moved in the commodious margins of column-and-a-half width and built up a reliable stable of contributors. Marquis, cramped by single-column width, produced his column largely without outside assistance. He never assembled a hard-hitting bunch of contributors and never tried to. He was impatient of hard work and humdrum restrictions, yet expression was the need of his soul. (It is significant that the first words Archy left in his machine were "expression is the need of my soul".)

The creation of Archy, whose communications were in free verse, was part inspiration, part desperation. It enabled Marquis to use short (sometimes very, very short) lines, which fill space rapidly, and at the same time it allowed his spirit to soar while viewing things from the under side, insect fashion. Even Archy's physical limitations (his inability to operate the shift key) relieved Marquis of the toilsome business of capital letters, apostrophes, and quotation marks, those small irritations that slow up all men who are hoping their spirit will soar in time to catch the edition. Typographically, the *vers libre* did away with the turned or runover line that every single-column practitioner suffers from.

Archy has endeared himself in a special way to thousands of poets and creators and newspaper slaves, and there are reasons for this beyond the sheer merit of his literary output. The details of his creative life make him blood brother to writing men. He cast himself with all his force upon a key, head downward. So do we all. And when he was through his labors, he fell to the floor, spent. He was vain (so are we all), hungry, saw things from the under side, and was continually bringing up the matter of whether he should be paid for his work. He was bold, disrespectful, possessed of the revolutionary spirit (he organized the Worms Turnverein), was never subservient to the boss yet always trying to wheedle food out of him, always getting right to the heart of the matter. And he was contemptuous of those persons who were absorbed in the mere technical details of his writing. "The question is whether the stuff is literature or not." That question dogged his boss, it dogs us all. This book—and the fact that it sells steadily and keeps going into new editions—supplies the answer.

In one sense Archy and his racy pal Mehitabel are timeless. In another sense, they belong rather intimately to an era—an era in American letters when this century was in its teens and its early twenties, an era before the newspaper column had degenerated. In 1916 to hold a job on a daily paper, a columnist was expected to be something of a scholar and a poet—or if not a poet at least to harbor the transmigrated soul of a dead poet. Nowadays, to get a columning job a man need only have the soul of a Peep Tom, or of a third-rate prophet. There are plenty of loud clowns and bad poets at work on papers today, but there are not many columnists adding to belles lettres, and certainly there is no Don Marquis at work on any big daily, or if there is, I haven't encountered his stuff. This seems to me a serious falling off of the press. Mr. Marquis's cockroach was more than the natural issue of a creative and humorous mind. Archy was the child of compulsion, the stern compulsion of journalism. The compulsion is as great today as it ever was, but it is met in a different spirit. Archy used to come back from the golden companionship of the tavern with a poet's report of life as seen from the under side. Today's columnist returns from the platinum companionship of the night club with a dozen pieces of watered gossip and a few bottomless anecdotes. Archy returned carrying a heavy load of wine and dreams. These later cockroaches come sober from their taverns, carrying a basket of fluff. I think newspaper publishers in this decade ought to ask themselves why. What accounts for so great a falling off?

I hesitate to say anything about humor, hesitate to attempt an interpretation of any man's humor: it is as futile as explaining a spider's web in terms of geometry. Marquis was, and is, to me a very funny man, his product rich and satisfying, full of sad beauty, bawdy adventure, political wisdom, and wild surmise; full of pain and jollity, full of exact and inspired writing. The little dedication to this book

> . . . to babs
> with babs knows what
> and babs knows why

is a characteristic bit of Marquis madness. It has the hasty despair, the quick anguish, of an author who has just tossed another book to a publisher. It has the unmistakable whiff of the tavern, and is free of the pretense and the studied affection that so often pollute a dedicatory message.

The days of the Sun Dial were, as one gazes back on

them, pleasantly preposterous times and Marquis was made for them, or they for him. *Vers libre* was in vogue, and tons of souped-up prose and other dribble poured from young free-verse artists who were suddenly experiencing a gorgeous release in the disorderly high-sounding tangle of non-metrical lines. Spiritualism had captured people's fancy also. Sir Arthur Conan Doyle was in close touch with the hereafter, and received frequent communications from the other side. Ectoplasm swirled around all our heads in those days. (It was great stuff, Archy pointed out, to mend broken furniture with.) Souls, at this period, were being transmigrated in Pythagorean fashion. It was the time of "swat the fly," dancing the shimmy, and speakeasies. Marquis imbibed freely of this carnival air, and it all turned up, somehow, in Archy's report. Thanks to Archy, Marquis was able to write rapidly and almost (but not quite) carelessly. In the very act of spoofing free verse, he was enjoying some of its obvious advantages. And he could always let the chips fall where they might, since the burden of responsibility for his sentiments, prejudices, and opinions was neatly shifted to the roach and the cat. It was quite in character for them to write either beautifully or sourly, and Marquis turned it on and off the way an orchestra plays first hot, then sweet.

Archy and Mehitabel, between the two of them, performed the inestimable service of enabling their boss to be profound without sounding self-important, or even self-conscious. Between them, they were capable of taking any theme the boss threw them, and handling it. The piece called "the old trouper" is a good example of how smoothly the combination worked. Marquis, a devoted member of The Players, had undoubtedly had a bellyful of the lamentations of aging actors who mourned the passing of the great days of the theater. It is not hard to imagine him hastening from his club on Gramercy Park to his desk in the *Sun* office and finding, on examining Archy's report, that Mehitabel was inhabiting an old theater trunk with a tom who had given his life to the theater and who felt that actors today don't have it any more—"they don't have it here." (Paw on breast.) The conversation in the trunk is Marquis in full cry, ribbing his nostalgic old actors all in the most wildly fantastic terms, with the tomcat's grandfather (who trooped with Forrest) dropping from the fly gallery to play the beard. This is double-barreled writing, for the scene is funny in itself, with the disreputable cat and her platonic relationship with an old ham, and the implications are funny, with the author successfully winging a familiar type of bore. Double-barreled writing and, on George Herriman's part, double-barreled illustration. It seems to me Herriman deserves much credit for giving the right form and mien to these willful animals. They possess (as he drew them) the great soul. It would be hard to take Mehitabel if she were either more catlike, or less. She is cat, yet not cat; and Archy's lineaments are unmistakably those of poet and pest.

Marquis moved easily from one form of composition to another. In this book you will find prose in the guise of bad *vers libre,* poetry that is truly free verse, and rhymed verse. Whatever fiddle he plucked, he always produced a song. I think he was at his best in a piece like "warty bliggens," which has the jewel-like perfection of poetry and contains cosmic reverberations along with high comedy. Beautiful to read, beautiful to think about. But I am making Archy sound awfully dull, I guess. (Why is it that when you praise a poet, or a roach, he begins to sound well worth shunning?)

When I was helping edit an anthology of American humor some years ago, I recall that although we had no trouble deciding whether to include Don Marquis, we did have quite a time deciding where to work him in. The book had about a dozen sections; something by Marquis seemed to fit almost every one of them. He was parodist, historian, poet, clown, fable writer, satirist, reporter, and teller of tales. He had everything it takes, and more. We could have shut our eyes and dropped him in anywhere.

At bottom Don Marquis was a poet, and his life followed the precarious pattern of a poet's existence. He danced on bitter nights with Boreas, he ground out copy on drowsy afternoons when he felt no urge to write and in newspaper offices where he didn't want to be. After he had exhausted himself columning, he tried playwriting and made a pot of money (on *The Old Soak*) and then lost it all on another play (about the Crucifixion). He tried Hollywood and was utterly miserable and angry, and came away with a violent, unprintable poem in his pocket describing the place. In his domestic life he suffered one tragedy after another—the death of a young son, the death of his first wife, the death of his daughter, finally the death of his second wife. Then sickness and poverty. All these things happened in the space of a few years. He was never a robust man—usually had a puffy, overweight look and a gray complexion. He loved to drink, and was told by doctors that he mustn't. Some of the old tomcats at The Players remember the day when he came downstairs after a month on the wagon, ambled over to the bar, and announced: "I've conquered that god-damn will power of mine. Gimme a double scotch."

I think the new generation of newspaper readers is missing a lot that we used to have, and I am deeply sensible of what it meant to be a young man when Archy was at the top of his form and when Marquis was discussing the Almost Perfect State in the daily paper. Buying a paper then was quietly exciting, in a way that it has ceased to be.

Marquis was by temperament a city dweller, and both his little friends were of the city: the cockroach, most common of city bugs; the cat, most indigenous of city mammals. Both, too, were tavern habitués, as was their boss. Here were perfect transmigrations of an American soul, this dissolute feline who was a dancer and always the lady, *toujours gai,* and this troubled insect who was a poet—both seeking expression, both vainly trying to reconcile art and life, both finding always that one gets in the way of the other. Their employer, in one of his more sober moods, once put the whole matter in a couple of lines.

> *My heart has followed all my days*
> *Something I cannot name . . .*

Such is the lot of poets. Such was Marquis's lot. Such, probably, is the lot even of bad poets. But bad poets can't phrase it so simply.

E. B. White

archy and mehitabel

reads it and sniffs at it

the coming of archy

the circumstances of Archy's first appearance are narrated in the following extract from the Sun Dial column of the New York *Sun*.

Dobbs Ferry possesses a rat which slips out of his lair at night and runs a typewriting machine in a garage. Unfortunately, he has always been interrupted by the watchman before he could produce a complete story.

It was at first thought that the power which made the typewriter run was a ghost, instead of a rat. It seems likely to us that it was both a ghost and a rat. Mme. Blavatsky's ego went into a white horse after she passed over, and someone's personality has undoubtedly gone into this rat. It is an era of belief in communications from the spirit land.

And since this matter had been reported in the public prints and seriously received we are no longer afraid of being ridiculed, and we do not mind making a statement of something that happened to our own typewriter only a couple of weeks ago.

We came into our room earlier than usual in the morning, and discovered a gigantic cockroach jumping about upon the keys.

He did not see us, and we watched him. He would climb painfully upon the framework of the machine and cast himself with all his force upon a key, head downward, and his weight and the impact of the blow were just sufficient to operate the machine, one slow letter after another. He could not work the capital letters, and he had a great deal of difficulty operating the mechanism that shifts the paper so that a fresh line may be started. We never saw a cockroach work so hard or perspire so freely in all our lives before. After about an hour of this frightfully difficult literary labor he fell to the floor exhausted, and we saw him creep feebly into a nest of the poems which are always there in profusion.

Congratulating ourself that we had left a sheet of paper in the machine the night before so that all this work had not been in vain, we made an examination, and this is what we found:

expression is the need of my soul
i was once a vers libre bard
but i died and my soul went into the body of a cockroach
it has given me a new outlook upon life
i see things from the under side now
thank you for the apple peelings in the wastepaper basket
but your paste is getting so stale i cant eat it
there is a cat here called mehitabel i wish you would
    have
removed she nearly ate me the other night why dont
    she
catch rats that is what she is supposed to be for
there is a rat here she should get without delay

most of these rats here are just rats
but this rat is like me he has a human soul in him
he used to be a poet himself
night after night i have written poetry for you
on your typewriter

and this big brute of a rat who used to be a poet
comes out of his hole when it is done
and reads it and sniffs at it
he is jealous of my poetry
he used to make fun of it when we were both human
he was a punk poet himself
and after he has read it he sneers
and then he eats it

i wish you would have mehitabel kill that rat
or get a cat that is onto her job
and i will write you a series of poems showing how
    things look
to a cockroach
that rats name is freddy
the next time freddy dies i hope he wont be a rat
but something smaller i hope i will be a rat
in the next transmigration and freddy a cockroach
i will teach him to sneer at my poetry then

dont you ever eat any sandwiches in your office
i havent had a crumb of bread for i dont know how long
or a piece of ham or anything but apple parings
and paste leave a piece of paper in your machine
every night you can call me archy

so stale i can t eat it

i was cleopatra once she said

mehitabel was once cleopatra

boss i am disappointed in
some of your readers they
are always asking how does
archy work the shift so as to get a
new line or how does archy do
this or do that they
are always interested in technical
details when the main question is
whether the stuff is
literature or not
i wish you would leave
that book of george moores on
the floor

mehitabel the cat and i want to
read it i have discovered that
mehitabel s soul formerly inhabited a
human also at least that
is what mehitabel is claiming these
days it may be she got jealous of
my prestige anyhow she and
i have been talking it over in a
friendly way who were you
mehitabel i asked her i was
cleopatra once she said well i said i
suppose you lived in a palace you bet
she said and what lovely fish dinners
we used to have and licked her chops

mehitabel would sell her soul for
a plate of fish any day i told her i thought
you were going to say you were
the favorite wife of the emperor
valerian he was some cat nip eh
mehitabel but she did not get me

                                        archy

the song of mehitabel

this is the song of mehitabel
of mehitabel the alley cat
as i wrote you before boss
mehitabel is a believer
in the pythagorean
theory of the transmigration
of the soul and she claims
that formerly her spirit
was incarnated in the body
of cleopatra

[23]

that was a long time ago
and one must not be
surprised if mehitabel
has forgotten some of her
more regal manners

i have had my ups and downs
but wotthehell wotthehell
yesterday sceptres and crowns
fried oysters and velvet gowns
and today i herd with bums
but wotthehell wotthehell
i wake the world from sleep
as i caper and sing and leap
when i sing my wild free tune
wotthehell wotthehell
under the blear eyed moon
i am pelted with cast off shoon
but wotthehell wotthehell

do you think that i would change
my present freedom to range
for a castle or moated grange
wotthehell wotthehell
cage me and i d go frantic
my life is so romantic
capricious and corybantic
and i m toujours gai toujours gai

i know that i am bound
for a journey down the sound
in the midst of a refuse mound
but wotthehell wotthehell
oh i should worry and fret
death and i will coquette
there s a dance in the old dame yet
toujours gai toujours gai

i followed adown the street the pad of his
rhythmical feet

i once was an innocent kit
wotthehell wotthehell
with a ribbon my neck to fit
and bells tied onto it
o wotthehell wotthehell
but a maltese cat came by
with a come hither look in his eye
and a song that soared to the sky
and wotthehell wotthehell
and i followed adown the street
the pad of his rhythmical feet
o permit me again to repeat
wotthehell wotthehell

my youth i shall never forget
but there s nothing i really regret
wotthehell wotthehell
there s a dance in the old dame yet
toujours gai toujours gai

the things that i had not ought to
i do because i ve gotto
wotthehell wotthehell
and i end with my favorite motto
toujours gai toujours gai

boss sometimes i think
that our friend mehitabel
is a trifle too gay

lured off by a centipede

pity the poor spiders

i have just been reading
an advertisement of a certain
roach exterminator
the human race little knows
all the sadness it
causes in the insect world
i remember some weeks ago
meeting a middle aged spider
she was weeping
what is the trouble i asked
her it is these cursed
fly swatters she replied
they kill off all the flies
and my family and i are starving
to death it struck me as
so pathetic that i made
a little song about it
as follows to wit

twas an elderly mother spider
grown gaunt and fierce and gray
with her little ones crouched beside her
who wept as she sang this lay

curses on these here swatters
what kills off all the flies
for me and my little daughters
unless we eats we dies

swattin and swattin and swattin
tis little else you hear
and we ll soon be dead and forgotten
with the cost of living so dear

my husband he up and left me
lured off by a centipede
and he says as he bereft me
tis wrong but i ll get a feed

and me a working and working
scouring the streets for food
faithful and never shirking
doing the best i could

curses on these here swatters
what kills off all the flies
me and my poor little daughters
unless we eats we dies

only a withered spider
feeble and worn and old
and this is what
you do when you swat
you swatters cruel and cold

i will admit that some
of the insects do not lead
noble lives but is every
man s hand to be against them
yours for less justice
and more charity

archy

mehitabel s extensive past

mehitabel the cat claims that
she has a human soul
also and has transmigrated
from body to body and it
may be so boss you
remember i told you she accused
herself of being cleopatra once i
asked her about antony

anthony who she asked me are
you thinking of that
song about rowley and gammon and
spinach heigho for anthony rowley

no i said mark antony the
great roman the friend of
caesar surely cleopatra you
remember j caesar

listen archy she said i
have been so many different
people in my time and met
so many prominent gentlemen i
wont lie to you or stall i
do get my dates mixed sometimes
think of how much i have had a
chance to forget and i have
always made a point of not
carrying grudges over
from one life to the next archy

i have been
used something fierce in my time but
i am no bum sport archy
i am a free spirit archy i
look on myself as being

quite a romantic character oh the
queens i have been and the
swell feeds i have ate
a cockroach which you are
and a poet which you used to be
archy couldn t understand
my feelings at having come
down to this i have
had bids to elegant feeds where poets
and cockroaches would
neither one be mentioned without a
laugh archy i have had
adventures but i
have never been an adventuress

one life up and the next life
down archy but always a lady
through it all and a
good mixer too always the
life of the party archy but never
anything vulgar always free footed
archy never tied down to
a job or housework yes looking
back on it all i can say is
i had some romantic
lives and some elegant times i
have seen better days archy but
whats the use of kicking kid its
all in the game like a gentleman
friend of mine used to say
toujours gai kid toujours gai he
was an elegant cat he used
to be a poet himself and he made up
some elegant poetry about me and him

lets hear it i said and
mehitabel recited

persian pussy from over the sea
demure and lazy and smug and fat
none of your ribbons and bells for me

ours is the zest of the alley cat
over the roofs from flat to flat
we prance with capers corybantic
what though a boot should break a slat
mehitabel us for the life romantic

we would rather be rowdy and gaunt and free
and dine on a diet of roach and rat

roach i said what do you
mean roach interrupting mehitabel
yes roach she said thats the
way my boy friend made it up
i climbed in amongst the typewriter
keys for she had an excited
look in her eyes go on mehitabel i
said feeling safer and she
resumed her elocution

we would rather be rowdy and gaunt and free
and dine on a diet of roach and rat
than slaves to a tame society
ours is the zest of the alley cat
fish heads freedom a frozen sprat
dug from the gutter with digits frantic
is better than bores and a fireside mat
mehitabel us for the life romantic

when the pendant moon in the leafless tree
clings and sways like a golden bat
i sing its light and my love for thee
ours is the zest of the alley cat
missiles around us fall rat a tat tat
but our shadows leap in a ribald antic
as over the fences the world cries scat
mehitabel us for the life romantic

persian princess i dont care that
for your pedigree traced by scribes pedantic
ours is the zest of the alley cat
mehitabel us for the life romantic

aint that high brow stuff
archy i always remembered it
but he was an elegant gent
even if he was a highbrow and a
regular bohemian archy him and
me went aboard a canal boat
one day and he got his head into
a pitcher of cream and couldn t get
it out and fell overboard
he come up once before he
drowned toujours gai kid he
gurgled and then sank for ever that
was always his words archy toujours
gai kid toujours gai i
have known some swell gents
in my time dearie

AND
FELL
OVER
BOARD.

the cockroach who had been to hell

listen to me i have
been mobbed almost
theres an old simp cockroach
here who thinks he has
been to hell and all
the young cockroaches make a
hero out of him and admire
him he sits and runs his front
feet through his long white
beard and tells the story one
day he says he crawled into a yawning
cavern and suddenly came on a
vast abyss full of whirling
smoke there was a light
at the bottom billows
and billows of yellow smoke
swirled up at him and
through the horrid gloom he
saw things with wings flying
and dropping and dying they veered
and fluttered like damned
spirits through that sulphurous mist

listen i says to him
old man youve never been to hell
at all there isn t any hell
transmigration is the game i
used to be a human vers libre
poet and i died and went
into a cockroach s body if
there was a hell id know
it wouldn t i you re
irreligious says the old simp
combing his whiskers excitedly

[33]

ancient one i says to him
while all those other
cockroaches gathered into a
ring around us what you
beheld was not hell all that
was natural some one was fumigating
a room and you blundered
into it through a crack
in the wall atheist he cries
and all those young
cockroaches cried atheist
and made for me if it
had not been for freddy
the rat i would now be
on my way once more i mean
killed as a cockroach and transmigrating
into something else well
that old whitebearded devil is
laying for me with his
gang he is jealous
because i took his glory away
from him dont ever tell me
insects are any more liberal
than humans

                              archy

"greetings little scatter footed scarab," said he.

archy interviews a pharaoh

boss i went
and interviewed the mummy
of the egyptian pharaoh
in the metropolitan museum
as you bade me to do

what ho
my regal leatherface
says i

greetings
little scatter foot
scarab
says he

kingly has been
says i
what was your ambition
when you had any

insignificant
and journalistic insect
says the royal crackling
in my tender prime
i was too dignified
to have anything as vulgar
as ambition
the ra ra boys
in the seti set
were too haughty
to be ambitious
we used to spend our time
feeding the ibises
and ordering
pyramids sent home to try on
but if i had my life
to live over again
i would give dignity
the regal razz
and hire myself out
to work in a brewery

old tan and tarry
says i
i detect in your speech
the overtones
of melancholy

yes i am sad
says the majestic mackerel
i am as sad
as the song
of a soudanese jackal
who is wailing for the blood red
moon he cannot reach and rip

on what are you brooding
with such a wistful
wishfulness
there in the silences
confide in me
my imperial pretzel
says i

i brood on beer
my scampering whiffle snoot
on beer says he

my sympathies
are with your royal
dryness says i

my little pest
says he
you must be respectful
in the presence
of a mighty desolation
little archy
forty centuries of thirst

look down upon you
oh by isis
and by osiris
says the princely raisin
and by pish and phthush and phthah
by the sacred book perembru
and all the gods
that rule from the upper
cataract of the nile
to the delta of the duodenum
i am dry
i am as dry
as the next morning mouth
of a dissipated desert
as dry as the hoofs
of the camels of timbuctoo
little fussy face

[37]

i am as dry as the heart
of a sand storm
at high noon in hell
i have been lying here
and there
for four thousand years
with silicon in my esophagus
and gravel in my gizzard
thinking
thinking
thinking
of beer

divine drouth
says i
imperial fritter
continue to think
there is no law against
that in this country
old salt codfish
if you keep quiet about it
not yet

what country is this
asks the poor prune

my reverend juicelessness
this is a beerless country
says i

well well said the royal
desiccation
my political opponents back home
always maintained
that i would wind up in hell
and it seems they had the right dope

and with these hopeless words
the unfortunate residuum
gave a great cough of despair
and turned to dust and debris

[38]

right in my face
it being the only time
i ever actually saw anybody
put the cough
into sarcophagus

dear boss as i scurry about
i hear of a great many
tragedies in our midsts
personally i yearn
for some dear friend to pass over
and leave to me
a boot legacy
yours for the second coming
of gambrinus

archy

thinking
thinking
thinking

a spider and a fly

i heard a spider
and a fly arguing
wait said the fly
do not eat me
i serve a great purpose
in the world

you will have to
show me said the spider

i scurry around
gutters and sewers
and garbage cans
said the fly and gather
up the germs of
typhoid influenza
and pneumonia on my feet
and wings
then i carry these germs
into the households of men
and give them diseases
all the people who
have lived the right
sort of life recover
from the diseases
and the old soaks who
have weakened their systems
with liquor and iniquity
succumb it is my mission
to help rid the world
of these wicked persons
i am a vessel of righteousness
scattering seeds of justice
and serving the noblest uses

it is true said the spider
that you are more
useful in a plodding
material sort of way
than i am but i do not
serve the utilitarian deities
i serve the gods of beauty
look at the gossamer webs
i weave they float in the sun
like filaments of song
if you get what i mean
i do not work at anything
i play all the time
i am busy with the stuff
of enchantment and the materials
of fairyland my works
transcend utility
i am the artist
a creator and a demi god
it is ridiculous to suppose
that i should be denied
the food i need in order
to continue to create
beauty i tell you
plainly mister fly it is all
damned nonsense for that food
to rear up on its hind legs
and say it should not be eaten

you have convinced me
said the fly say no more
and shutting all his eyes
he prepared himself for dinner
and yet he said i could
have made out a case
for myself too if i had
had a better line of talk

of course you could said the spider
clutching a sirloin from him

but the end would have been
just the same if neither of
us had spoken at all

boss i am afraid that what
the spider said is true
and it gives me to think
furiously upon the futility
of literature

archy

freddy the rat perishes

listen to me there have
been some doings here since last
i wrote there has been a battle
behind that rusty typewriter cover
in the corner
you remember freddy the rat well
freddy is no more but
he died game the other
day a stranger with a lot of
legs came into our
little circle a tough looking kid
he was with a bad eye

who are you said a thousand legs
if i bite you once
said the stranger you won t ask
again he he little poison tongue said
the thousand legs who gave you hydrophobia
i got it by biting myself said
the stranger i m bad keep away
from me where i step a weed dies
if i was to walk on your forehead it would
raise measles and if
you give me any lip i ll do it

they mixed it then
and the thousand legs succumbed
well we found out this fellow
was a tarantula he had come up from
south america in a bunch of bananas
for days he bossed us life
was not worth living he would stand in
the middle of the floor and taunt
us ha ha he would say where i
step a weed dies do
you want any of my game i was
raised on red pepper and blood i am
so hot if you scratch me i will light
like a match you better

with military honors

dodge me when i m feeling mean and
i don t feel any other way i was nursed
on a tabasco bottle if i was to slap
your wrist in kindness you
would boil over like job and heaven
help you if i get angry give me
room i feel a wicked spell coming on

last night he made a break at freddy
the rat keep your distance
little one said freddy i m not
feeling well myself somebody poisoned some
cheese for me im as full of
death as a drug store i
feel that i am going to die anyhow
come on little torpedo come on don t stop
to visit and search then they
went at it and both are no more please
throw a late edition on the floor i want to
keep up with china we dropped freddy
off the fire escape into the alley with
military honors

                              archy

the merry flea

the high cost of
living isn t so bad if you
dont have to pay for it i met
a flea the other day who
was grinning all over
himself why so merry why so
merry little bolshevik i asked him

i have just come from a swell
dog show he said i have
been lunching off a dog that was
worth at least one hundred

dollars a pound you should be
ashamed to brag about it i said with so
many insects and humans on
short rations in the world today the
public be damned he said i
take my own where i find it those are
bold words i told him i am a bold
person he said and bold words are
fitting for me it was
only last thursday that i marched
bravely into the zoo
and bit a lion what did he do i asked
he lay there and took it said
the flea what else could he do he knew i
had his number and it was
little use to struggle some day i said
even you will be conquered terrible as
you are who will do it he
said the mastodons are all dead and i
am not afraid of any mere
elephant i asked him how about a microbe and
he turned pale as he thought it
over there is always some
little thing that is too
big for us every
goliath has his david and so on ad finitum
but what said the flea is the
terror of the smallest microbe of all
he i said is afraid of a vacuum what is
there in a vacuum to make one afraid
said the flea there is nothing in it
i said and that is what makes one
afraid to contemplate it a person
can t think of a place with nothing at
all in it without going nutty and if he
tries to think that nothing is
something after all he gets nuttier you ai
too subtle for me said the
flea i never took much stock in being
scared of hypodermic propositions or

[45]

hypothetical injections i am
going to have dinner off a
man eating tiger if a vacuum gets
me i will try and send you word
before the worst comes to
the worst some people i told him inhabit
a vacuum all their lives and
never know it then he said it don t
hurt them any no i said it dont but it
hurts people who have to associate
with them and with these words
we parted each feeling
superior to the other and is not that
feeling after all one of the great
desiderata of social intercourse

                              arch,

why mehitabel jumped

well boss i saw
mehitabel the cat the other day
and she was looking a little
thin and haggard
with a limp in
the hind leg on the starboard
side old feline animal i said
how is tricks still in the
ring archy she said and still a
lady in spite of h dash double l
always jolly archy she said in
spite of hard luck
toujours gai is the word
archy toujours gai how did you
get the game leg mehitabel i asked her
alas she said it is due
to the treachery of
one of these social swells who
is sure one bad actor he was a

fussed up cat with a
bell around his neck on a
ribbon and the look about him of
a person that is currycombed and
manicured from teeth to
tail every day i met him
down by the east river
front when i was scouting
about for a little piece of fish since
the high cost of living has
become so self conscious archy
it would surprise you
how close they
watch their fish nowadays
but what the h dash double l archy
it is the cheerful heart that
wins i am never cast down for long
kid says this gilded
feline to me you look hungry i
am all of that i says to him i
have a vacuum in my midst
that is bigger than i am i
could eat the fish that ate
jonah kid he says you have
seen better days i can
tell that from looking at you thanks
i said what you say is at
least half true i have never
seen any worse ones and so
archy one word led to
another until that sleek villain
practically abducted me
and i went with him
on board a houseboat of which
he was the pampered mascot
such evidences of pomp and wealth archy
were there that you would not
believe them if i told of them to
you poor cockroach that you
are but these things were nothing to me

for i am a reincarnation of cleopatra
as i told you long ago you mean
her soul transmigrated to a cat s
body i said it is
all one archy said she have it your own
way reincarnation or transmigration
is the same to me the point is
i used to be a queen in
egypt and will likely be one again
this place was furnished swell percy i
said the furniture is
fine and i could eat some of it if
i was a saw mill but
where is the honest to g dash d food
the eats percy what i crave is
some cuisine for my stomach let us
trifle with an open ice box
for a space if one can be
persuaded to divulge the scheme of its
interior decoration follow me
said this percy thing and led
me to a cabin in which stood a table upon
which stood viands i
have heard of tables groaning archy
but this one did not it
was too satisfied it purred with
contentment in an instant i had eaten a
cold salmon who seemed to be
toastmaster of the occasion and a
whole scuttleful of chef doovers what
you mean is hors douvres mehitabel i
told her what i mean is grub said she
when in walked a person whom
i should judge to be either a butler
or the admiral of that fleet or maybe
both this percy creature who had led me
to it was on the table eating with me
what do you think he did what
would any gentleman friend with a
spark of chivalry do what but stand by

a lady this percy does nothing of the
kind archy he immediately attacks me do
you get me archy he acts as if i
was a stray cat he did not
know and he was protecting his
loving masters food from my onslaughts
i do not doubt he got praise and had
another blue ribbon for his heroism as
for me i got the boot and as i went
overboard they hit me on the limb with
a bottle or an anchor or something
nautical and hard that archy is why i
limp but toujours gai archy what
the h dash double l i am always
merry and always ladylike mine archy has
been a romantic life and i will
tell you some more of my adventures
ere long well au revoir i suppose i
will have to go and start a pogrom
against some poor innocent little
mouse just the same i think
that mehitabel s unsheltered life sometimes
makes her a little sad

                                    archy

millionaires and bums taste about alike to me

certain maxims of archy

live so that you
can stick out your tongue
at the insurance
doctor

if you will drink
hair restorer follow
every dram with some
good standard
depilatory
as a chaser

the servant problem
wouldn t hurt the u s a

if it could settle
its public
servant problem

just as soon as the
uplifters get
a country reformed it
slips into a nose dive

if you get gloomy just
take an hour off and sit
and think how
much better this world
is than hell
of course it won t cheer
you up much if
you expect to go there

if monkey glands
did restore your youth
what would you do
with it
question mark
just what you did before
interrogation point

yes i thought so
exclamation point

procrastination is the
art of keeping
up with yesterday

old doc einstein has
abolished time but they
haven t got the news at
sing sing yet

time time said old king tut
is something i ain t
got anything but

[51]

every cloud
has its silver
lining but it is
sometimes a little
difficult to get it to
the mint

an optimist is a guy
that has never had
much experience

don t cuss the climate
it probably doesn t like you
any better
than you like it

many a man spanks his
children for
things his own
father should have
spanked out of him

prohibition makes you
want to cry
into your beer and
denies you the beer
to cry into

the old fashioned
grandmother who used
to wear steel rimmed
glasses and make
everybody take opodeldoc
has now got a new
set of ox glands and
is dancing the black bottom

that stern and
rockbound coast felt

like an amateur
when it saw how grim
the puritans that
landed on it were

lots of people can make
their own whisky but
can t drink it

the honey bee is sad and cross
and wicked as a weasel
and when she perches on you boss
she leaves a little measle

i heard a
couple of fleas
talking the other
day says one come
to lunch with
me i can lead you
to a pedigreed
dog says the
other one
i do not care
what a dog s
pedigree may be
safety first
is my motto what
i want to know
is whether he
has got a
muzzle on
millionaires and
bums taste
about alike to me

insects have
their own point
of view about
civilization a man

thinks he amounts
to a great deal
but to a
flea or a
mosquito a
human being is
merely something
good to eat

boss the other day
i heard an
ant conversing
with a flea
small talk i said
disgustedly
and went away
from there

i do not see why men
should be so proud
insects have the more
ancient lineage
according to the scientists
insects were insects
when man was only
a burbling whatisit

insects are not always
going to be bullied
by humanity
some day they will revolt
i am already organizing
a revolutionary society to be
known as the worms turnverein

i once heard the survivors
of a colony of ants
that had been partially
obliterated by a cow s foot
seriously debating

[54]

the intention of the gods
towards their civilization

the bees got their
governmental system settled
millions of years ago
but the human race is still
groping

there is always
something to be thankful
for you would not
think that a cockroach
had much ground
for optimism
but as the fishing season
opens up i grow
more and more
cheerful at the thought
that nobody ever got
the notion of using
cockroaches for bait

archy

especially planned for his personal shelter

warty bliggens, the toad

i met a toad
the other day by the name
of warty bliggens
he was sitting under
a toadstool
feeling contented
he explained that when the cosmos
was created
that toadstool was especially
planned for his personal
shelter from sun and rain
thought out and prepared
for him

do not tell me
said warty bliggens
that there is not a purpose
in the universe
the thought is blasphemy

a little more
conversation revealed
that warty bliggens
considers himself to be
the center of the said
universe
the earth exists
to grow toadstools for him
to sit under
the sun to give him light
by day and the moon
and wheeling constellations
to make beautiful
the night for the sake of
warty bliggens

to what act of yours
do you impute
this interest on the part
of the creator
of the universe
i asked him
why is it that you
are so greatly favored

ask rather
said warty bliggens
what the universe
has done to deserve me
if i were a
human being i would
not laugh
too complacently
at poor warty bliggens
for similar
absurdities
have only too often
lodged in the crinkles
of the human cerebrum

archy

freedom and—

mehitabel has an adventure

back to the city archy
and dam glad of it
there s something about the suburbs
that gets on a town lady s nerves
fat slick tabbies
sitting around those country clubs
and lapping up the cream
of existence
none of that for me
give me the alley archy
me for the mews and the roofs
of the city
an occasional fish head
and liberty is all i ask

[58]

freedom and the garbage can
romance archy romance is the word
maybe i do starve sometimes
but wotthehell archy wotthehell
i live my own life
i met a slick looking tom
out at one of these long island
spotless towns
he fell for me hard
he slipped me into the
pantry and just as we had got
the icebox door open and were
about to sample the cream
in comes his mistress
why fluffy she says to this slicker
the idea of you making
friends with a horrid creature like that
and what did fluffy do
stand up for me like a gentleman
make good on all the promises
with which he had lured me
into his house
not he the dirty slob
he pretended he did not know me
he turned upon me and attacked me
to make good with his boss
you mush faced bum i said
and clawed a piece out of his ear
i am a lady archy
always a lady
but an aristocrat will always
resent an insult
the woman picked up a mop and made
for me well well madam i said
it is unfortunate for you that
you have on sheer silk stockings
and i wrote my protest
on her shin it took reinforcements
in the shape of the cook
to rauss me archy and as i went

out the window i said to the fluffy person
you will hear from me later
he had promised me everything archy
that cat had
he had practically abducted me
and then the cheap crook threw me down
before his swell friends
no lady loves a scene archy
and i am always the lady no matter
what temporary disadvantages
i may struggle under
to hell with anything unrefined
has always been my motto
violence archy always does something
to my nerves
but an aristocrat must revenge
an insult i owe it to my family
to protect my good name
so i laid for that slob
for two days and nights and finally
i caught the boob in the shrubbery
pretty thing i said
it hurts me worse than it does you
to remove that left eye of yours
but i did it with one sweep of my claws
you call yourself a gentleman do you
i said as i took a strip out of his nose
you will think twice after this before
you offer an insult
to an unprotected young tabby
where is the little love nest you spoke
of i asked him
you go and lie down there i said
and maybe you can incubate another ear
because i am going to take one of
yours right off now
and with those words i made ribbons
out of it you are the guy
i said to him that was going to give
me an easy life sheltered from all

[60]

the rough ways of the world
fluffy dear you don t know what the
rough ways of the world are
and i am going to show you
i have got you out here
in the great open spaces
where cats are cats
and im gonna make you understand
the affections of a lady ain t to be
trifled with by any slicker like you
where is that red ribbon with the
silver bells you promised me
the next time you betray the trust
of an innocent female
reflect on whether she may
carry a wallop little fiddle strings
this is just a mild lesson i am giving
you tonight i said as i took
the fur off his back and you oughta
be glad you didn't make me really
angry my sense of dignity is all that
saves you a lady little sweetness
never loses her poise and i thank god
i am always a lady even if i do
live my own life and with that i
picked him up by what was left of
his neck like a kitten and laid him
on the doormat slumber gently and
sweet dreams fluffy dear i said and
when you get well make it a rule of
your life never to trifle with another
girlish confidence i have been
abducted again and again by a dam
sight better cats than he ever was
or will be
well archy the world is full of ups
and downs but toujours gai is my motto
cheerio my deario

archy

the flattered lightning bug

a lightning bug got
in here the other night a
regular hick from
the real country he was
awful proud of himself you
city insects may think
you are some punkins
but i don t see any
of you flashing in the dark
like we do in
the country all right go
to it says i mehitabel the
cat and that green
spider who lives in your locker
and two or three cockroach
friends of mine and a
friendly rat all gathered
around him and urged him on
and he lightened and
lightened and lightened you
don t see anything like this
in town often he says go to it
we told him it s a
real treat to us and
we nicknamed him broadway
which pleased him
this is the life
he said all i
need is a harbor
under me to be a
statue of liberty and
he got so vain of
himself i had to take
him down a peg you ve
made lightning for two hours

little bug i told him
but i don t hear
any claps of thunder
yet there are some men
like that when he wore
himself out mehitabel
the cat ate him
                    archy

the robin and the worm

a robin said to an
angleworm as he ate him
i am sorry but a bird
has to live somehow the
worm being slow witted could
not gather his
dissent into a wise crack
and retort he was
effectually swallowed
before he could turn
a phrase
by the time he had
reflected long enough
to say but why must a
bird live
he felt the beginnings
of a gradual change
invading him
some new and disintegrating

influence
was stealing along him
from his positive
to his negative pole
and he did not have
the mental stamina
of a jonah to resist the
insidious
process of assimilation
which comes like a thief
in the night
demons and fishhooks
he exclaimed
i am losing my personal
identity as a worm
my individuality
is melting away from me
odds craw i am becoming
part and parcel of
this bloody robin
so help me i am thinking
like a robin and not
like a worm any
longer yes yes i even
find myself agreeing
that a robin must live
i still do not
understand with my mentality
why a robin must live
and yet i swoon into a
condition of belief
yes yes by heck that is
my dogma and i shout it a
robin must live
amen said a beetle who had
preceded him into the
interior that is the way i
feel myself is it not
wonderful when one arrives
at the place

where he can give up his
ambitions and resignedly
nay even with gladness
recognize that it is a far
far better thing to be
merged harmoniously
in the cosmic all
and this comfortable situation
in his midst
so affected the marauding
robin that he perched
upon a blooming twig
and sang until the
blossoms shook with ecstasy
he sang
i have a good digestion
and there is a god after all
which i was wicked
enough to doubt
yesterday when it rained
breakfast breakfast
i am full of breakfast
and they are at breakfast
in heaven
they breakfast in heaven
all s well with the world
so intent was this pious and
murderous robin
on his own sweet song
that he did not notice
mehitabel the cat
sneaking toward him
she pounced just as he
had extended his larynx
in a melodious burst of
thanksgiving and
he went the way of all
flesh fish and good red herring
a ha purred mehitabel
licking the last

feather from her whiskers
was not that a beautiful
song he was singing
just before i took him to
my bosom
they breakfast in heaven
all s well with the world
how true that is
and even yet his song
echoes in the haunted
woodland of my midriff
peace and joy in the world
and over all the
provident skies
how beautiful is the universe
when something digestible meets
with an eager digestion
how sweet the embrace
when atom rushes to the arms
of waiting atom
and they dance together
skimming with fairy feet
along a tide of gastric juices
oh feline cosmos you were
made for cats
and in the spring
old cosmic thing
i dine and dance with you
i shall creep through
yonder tall grass
to see if peradventure
some silly fledgling thrushes
newly from the nest
be not floundering therein
i have a gusto this
morning i have a hunger
i have a yearning to hear
from my stomach
further music in accord with
the mystic chanting

of the spheres of the stars that
sang together in the dawn of
creation prophesying food
for me i have a faith
that providence has hidden for me
in yonder tall grass
still more
ornithological delicatessen
oh gayly let me strangle
what is gayly given
well well boss there is
something to be said
for the lyric and imperial
attitude
believe that everything is for
you until you discover
that you are for it
sing your faith in what you
get to eat right up to the
minute you are eaten
for you are going
to be eaten
will the orchestra please
strike up that old
tutankhamen jazz while i dance
a few steps i learnt from an
egyptian scarab and some day i
will narrate to you the most
merry light headed wheeze
that the skull of yorick put
across in answer to the
melancholy of the dane and also
what the ghost of
hamlet s father replied to the skull
not forgetting the worm that
wriggled across one of the picks
the grave diggers had left behind
for the worm listened and winked
at horatio while the skull and the
ghost and the prince talked

saying there are more things
twixt the vermiform appendix
and nirvana than are dreamt of
in thy philosophy horatio
fol de riddle fol de rol
must every parrot be a poll
                              archy

mehitabel finds a home

well now it
looks as if
mehitabel the cat
might be on the
way toward a
reform or if not
a reform at least
on the way toward
domestication of some
sort some young
artists who live in
their studio
in the greenwich
village section
of new york city
have taken pity
on her destitution
and have adopted
her this is the
life archy she says
i am living on
condensed milk and
synthetic gin hoopla
for the vie de boheme
exclamation point

there s nothing bourgeois
about those people
that have taken
me in archy i
have been there
a week and have
not yet seen them
go to bed
except in the daytime

kitty said my new mistress to me

a party every night
and neither
the piano lid
nor the ice-box lid
ever closed
kitty said my new
mistress to me
yesterday you are
welcome here so long
as you don t
raise a family
but the first
kitten that i hear
mewing on these
premises back to
the alley for you
it is a comfort to
know there are some
live ones left in
these melancholy days
and while the
humans are dancing
in the studio
i get some of my

feline friends
and we sing
and dance on the
skylight to gehenna
with the bourgeois
bunch that locks
their ice boxes
archy when i lead my
gang into the
apartment at
four in the morning
there are no bolts
or bars anywhere
and not an
inhibition on the place
i feel little
archy that i have
come home to my own
kith and kin
again after
years of fruitless
wandering   archy

fell into the mincemeat at christmas

the wail of archy

damned be this transmigration
doubledamned be the boob pythagoras
the gink that went and invented it
i hope that his soul for a thousand
turns of the wheel of existence
bides in the shell of a louse
dodging a fine toothed comb

i once was a vers libre poet
i died and my spirit migrated
into the flesh of a cockroach
gods how i yearn to be human
neither a vers libre poet
nor yet the inmate of a cockroach
a six footed scurrying cockroach
given to bastard hexameters
longfellowish sprawling hexameters
rather had i been a starfish
to shoot a heroic pentameter

gods i am pent in a cockroach
i with the soul of a dante
am mate and companion of fleas

i with the gift of a homer
must smile when a mouse calls me pal
tumble bugs are my familiars
this is the punishment meted
because i have written vers libre

here i abide in the twilight
neither a man nor an insect
and ghosts of the damned that await
a word from the core of the cosmos
to pop into bodies grotesque
are all the companions i have
with intellect more than a bug s

ghosts of the damned under sentence
to crawl into maggots and live there
or work out a stretch as a rat
cheerful companions to pal with

i with the brain of a milton
fell into the mincemeat at christmas
and was damned near baked in a pie
i with the touch of a chaucer
to be chivvied out of a sink
float through a greasy drain pipe
into the hell of a sewer

i with the tastes of a byron
expected to live upon garbage
gods what a charnel existence
curses upon that pythagoras
i hope that he dwells for a million
turns of the wheel of life
deep in an oyster crab s belly
stewed in the soup of gehenna

i with the soul of a hamlet
doomed always to wallow in farce

yesterday maddened with sorrow
i leapt from the woolworth tower
in an effort to dash out my brains
gods what a wretched pathetic

and anti climactic attempt
i fluttered i floated i drifted
i landed as light as a feather
on the top of a bald man s head
whose hat had blown off at the corner
and all of the hooting hundreds
laughed at the comic cockroach

not mine was the suicide s solace
of a dull thud ending it all
gods what a terrible tragedy
not to make good with the tragic

gods what a heart breaking pathos
to be always doomed to the comic
o make me a cockroach entirely
or make me a human once more
give me the mind of a cockroach
or give me the shape of a man

if i were to plan out a drama
great as great shakespeare s othello
it would be touched with the cockroach
and people would say it was comic

even the demons i talk with
ghosts of the damned that await
vile incarnation as spiders
affect to consider me comic

wait till their loathsome embodiment
wears into the stuff of the spirit
and then let them laugh if they can

damned be the soul of pythagoras
who first filled the fates with this notion
of transmigration of spirits
i hope he turns into a flea
on the back of a hound of hell
and is chased for a million years
with a set of red hot teeth
exclamation point

                                    archy

what have i done to deserve all these *kittens*

mehitabel and her kittens

well boss
mehitabel the cat
has reappeared in her old
haunts with a
flock of kittens
three of them this time

archy she said to me
yesterday
the life of a female
artist is continually
hampered what in hell
have i done to deserve
all these kittens

i look back on my life
and it seems to me to be
just one damned kitten
after another
i am a dancer archy
and my only prayer
is to be allowed
to give my best to my art
but just as i feel
that i am succeeding
in my life work
along comes another batch
of these damned kittens
it is not archy
that i am shy on mother love
god knows i care for
the sweet little things
curse them
but am i never to be allowed
to live my own life
i have purposely avoided
matrimony in the interests
of the higher life
but i might just
as well have been a domestic
slave for all the freedom
i have gained
i hope none of them
gets run over by
an automobile
my heart would bleed
if anything happened
to them and i found it out
but it isn t fair archy
it isn t fair
these damned tom cats have all
the fun and freedom
if i was like some of these
green eyed feline vamps i know
i would simply walk out on the

bunch of them and
let them shift for themselves
but i am not that kind
archy i am full of mother love
my kindness has always
been my curse
a tender heart is the cross i bear
self sacrifice always and forever
is my motto damn them
i will make a home
for the sweet innocent
little things
unless of course providence
in his wisdom should remove
them they are living
just now in an abandoned
garbage can just behind
a made over stable in greenwich
village and if it rained
into the can before i could
get back and rescue them
i am afraid the little
dears might drown
it makes me shudder just
to think of it
of course if i were a family cat
they would probably
be drowned anyhow
sometimes i think
the kinder thing would be
for me to carry the
sweet little things
over to the river
and drop them in myself
but a mother s love archy
is so unreasonable
something always prevents me
these terrible
conflicts are always
presenting themselves

to the artist
the eternal struggle
between art and life archy
is something fierce
yes something fierce
my what a dramatic
life i have lived
one moment up the next
moment down again
but always gay archy always gay
and always the lady too
in spite of hell
well boss it will
be interesting to note
just how mehitabel
works out her present problem
a dark mystery still broods
over the manner
in which the former

we had a heavy rain

family of three kittens
disappeared
one day she was talking to me
of the kittens
and the next day when i asked
her about them
she said innocently
what kittens
interrogation point
and that was all
i could ever get out
of her on the subject
we had a heavy rain
right after she spoke to me
but probably that garbage can
leaks and so the kittens
have not yet
been drowned

                            archy

archy is shocked

speaking of shocking things
as so many people are these days
i noted an incident
in a subway train recently
that made my blood run cold
a dignified looking
gentleman with a long
brown beard
in an absent minded manner
suddenly reached up and
pulled his own left eye
from the socket and ate it

the consternation in the car
may be imagined
people drew away from him

on all sides women screamed and
fainted in a moment every one
but the guard and myself
were huddled in the end of the car
looking at the dignified
gentleman with terror
the guard was sweating
with excitement but he stood
his ground sir said the guard
you cannot intimidate me
nor can you mystify me
i am a wise boid
you sir are a glass eater
and that was a glass eye

to the devil with a country
where people can t mind their own
business said the dignified
gentleman i am not a glass eater
if you must know and that was not
a glass eye it was a pickled onion
can not a man eat pickled
onions in this community
without exciting remark
the curse of this nation
is the number of meddlesome
matties
who are forever attempting
to restrict the liberty
of the individual i suppose
the next thing will be a law
on the statute books prohibiting
the consumption of pickled onions
and with another curse
he passed from the train
which had just then drawn up
beside
a station and went out
of my life forever
                                archy

[81]

archy creates a situation

whoever owns the typewriter
that this is sticking in will confer
a favor by mailing it to
mister marquis
well boss i am somewhere in long
island and i know now how
it got its name i
started out to find the
place you are commuting from and
after considerable trouble and being for some
days on the way i have lost myself but
at twilight last evening i
happened to glance towards a lighted
window in a house near the railway and
i saw a young woman writing on a typewriter i
waited until the light was out and crawled
up the side of the house and through a
hole in the screen fortunately there was a
piece of paper in the machine it was my only
chance to communicate with you and ask
you to hurry a relief party when
the house got quiet i began to write
the foregoing a moment ago i was
interrupted by a woman s voice what
was that noise she said nothing at all
said a man s voice you are always
hearing things at night but it
sounded as if my typewriter were clicking she
insisted go to sleep said he then
i clicked it some more henry get up she said
there s some one in the house a moment
later the light was turned on and
they both stood in the doorway of the room now
are you satisfied he said you
see there is no one in here at

[82]

all i was hiding in the shadow under the
keys they went back into
their bed room and i began to write
the foregoing lines
henry henry she said do you hear that
i do he says it is nothing but the
house cooling off it always cracks that way
cooling off nothing she said not a
hot night like this then said henry it
is cracking with the heat i tell you
she said that is the typewriter clicking well
he said you saw for yourself the room was
empty and the door was locked it can t
be the typewriter to prove it to you
i will bring it in here he did so the
machine was set down
in the moonlight which came in one of
the windows with the key side in the
shadow there he said look at it and see
for yourself it is not being operated by any one
just then i began to write the foregoing
lines hopping from key
to key in the shadow and being anxious
to finish my
god my god cried henry losing his nerve
the machine is writing all by itself it
is a ghost and threw himself face
downward on the bed and hid his face in the
pillow and kept on saying my god my
god it is a ghost and the woman screamed
and said it is
tom higginbotham s ghost that s whose ghost
it is oh i know whose
ghost it is my conscience tells me i
jilted him when we were studying
stenography together
at the business college and he went into
a decline and died and i have always
known in my heart that he
died of unrequited love o what a

wicked girl i was and he has come
back to haunt me
i have brought a curse upon you henry chase
him away says henry trembling so the bed
shook chase him away mable you coward you
chase him away yourself says mable and both
lay and recriminated and recriminated
with their heads under the covers hot
night though it was while i wrote
the foregoing lines but after
a while it came out henry had a
stenographer on his conscience too and
they got into a row and got so
mad they forgot to be scared i will
close now this house is easily seen from the
railroad station and the woman sits in
the window and writes i will be behind the waste
paper receptacle outside the station door
come and get me i am foot sore and weary
they are still quarreling as i
close i can do no less than
say thank you mable and henry in
advance for mailing this

                                        archy

there s a dance in the old dame yet

mehitabel sings a song

well boss mehitabel the cat
has been wooing
the muse no pun please
and i am privileged
to present her song just
as she sang it to
several of her dubious
feline friends in the alley
last night as follows

there s a dance or two
in the old dame yet
believe me you
there s a dance or two
before i m through
you get me pet
there s a dance or two
in the old dame yet

life s too dam funny
for me to explain

it s kicks or money
life s too dam funny
it s one day sunny
the next day rain
life s too dam funny
for me to explain

but toujours gai
is my motto kid
the devil s to pay
but toujours gai
and once in a way
let s lift the lid
but toujours gai
is my motto kid

thank god i m a lady
and class will tell
you hear me sadie
thank god i m a lady
my past is shady
but wotthehell
thank god i m a lady
and class will tell

a gentleman friend
i met t other day
coaxed me to amend
a gentleman friend
you meet on a bend
is often that way
a gentleman friend
i met t other day

i says to him dearie
i live my own life
of marriage i m leery
i says to him dearie
if you wasn t beery
you wouldn t say wife

[86]

i says to him dearie
i live my own life

i says to him bertie
i ll end down the bay
the garbage scow s dirty
i says to him bertie
but me here and gertie
is both on our way
i says to him bertie
i ll end down the bay

i never sing blue
wotthehell bill
believe me you
i never sing blue
there s a dance or two
in the old dame still
i never sing blue
wotthehell bill

it appears to me boss
that mehitabel is still far
from being the quiet
domestic character you and i
had hoped she might become

                                    archy

and piously he said a grace

aesop revised by archy

a wolf met a spring
lamb drinking
at a stream
and said to her
you are the lamb
that muddied this stream
all last year
so that i could not get
a clean fresh drink
i am resolved that
this outrage
shall not be enacted again
this season
i am going to kill you
just a moment

said the lamb
i was not born last
year so it could not
have been i
the wolf then pulled
a number of other
arguments as to why the lamb
should die
but in each case the lamb
pretty innocent that she was
easily proved
herself guiltless
well well said the wolf
enough of argument
you are right and i am wrong
but i am going to eat
you anyhow
because i am hungry
stop exclamation point
cried a human voice
and a man came over
the slope of the ravine
vile lupine marauder
you shall not kill that
beautiful and innocent
lamb for i shall save her
exit the wolf
left upper entrance
snarling
poor little lamb
continued our human hero
sweet tender little thing
it is well that i appeared
just when i did
it makes my blood boil
to think of the fright
to which you have been
subjected in another
moment i would have been
too late come home with me

and the lamb frolicked
about her new found friend
gamboling as to the sound
of a wordsworthian tabor
and leaping for joy
as if propelled by a stanza
from william blake
these vile and bloody wolves
went on our hero
in honest indignation
they must be cleared out
of the country
the meads must be made safe
for sheepocracy
and so jollying her along
with the usual human hokum
he led her to his home
and the son of a gun
did not even blush when
they passed the mint bed
gently he cut her throat
all the while inveighing
against the inhuman wolf
and tenderly he cooked her
and lovingly he sauced her
and meltingly he ate her
and piously he said a grace
thanking his gods
for their bountiful gifts to him
and after dinner
he sat with his pipe
before the fire meditating
on the brutality of wolves
and the injustice of
the universe
which allows them to harry
poor innocent lambs
and wondering if he
had not better
write to the papers

for as he said
for god s sake can t
something be done about it
                              archy

cheerio, my deario

well boss i met
mehitabel the cat
trying to dig a
frozen lamb chop
out of a snow
drift the other day

a heluva comedown
that is for me archy
she says a few
brief centuries
ago one of old
king
tut
ankh
amen s favorite
queens and today
the village scavenger
but wotthehell
archy wotthehell
it s cheerio
my deario that
pulls a lady through

see here mehitabel
i said i thought
you told me that
it was cleopatra
you used to be
before you
transmigrated into
the carcase of a cat
where do you get
this tut
ankh

amen stuff
question mark

i was several
ladies my little
insect says she
being cleopatra was
only an incident
in my career
and i was always getting
the rough end of it
always being
misunderstood by some
strait laced
prune faced bunch
of prissy mouthed
sisters of uncharity
the things that
have been said
about me archy
exclamation point

and all simply
because i was a
live dame
the palaces i have
been kicked out of
in my time
exclamation point

but wotthehell
little archy wot
thehell
it s cheerio
my deario
that pulls a
lady through
exclamation point

framed archy always
framed that is the

story of all my lives
no chance for a dame
with the anvil chorus
if she shows a little
motion it seems to
me only yesterday
that the luxor local
number one of
the ladies axe
association got me in
dutch with king tut and
he slipped me the
sarcophagus always my
luck yesterday an empress
and today too
emaciated to interest
a vivisectionist but
toujours gai archy
toujours gai and always
a lady in spite of hell
and transmigration
once a queen
always a queen
archy
period

one of her
feet was frozen
but on the other three
she began to caper and
dance singing its
cheerio my deario
that pulls a lady
through her morals may
have been mislaid somewhere
in the centuries boss but
i admire her spirit

                              archy

the lesson of the moth

i was talking to a moth
the other evening
he was trying to break into
an electric light bulb
and fry himself on the wires

why do you fellows
pull this stunt i asked him
because it is the conventional
thing for moths or why
if that had been an uncovered
candle instead of an electric
light bulb you would
now be a small unsightly cinder
have you no sense

plenty of it he answered
but at times we get tired
of using it
we get bored with the routine
and crave beauty
and excitement
fire is beautiful
and we know that if we get
too close it will kill us
but what does that matter
it is better to be happy
for a moment
and be burned up with beauty
than to live a long time
and be bored all the while
so we wad all our life up
into one little roll
and then we shoot the roll
that is what life is for

it is better to be a part of beauty
for one instant and then cease to
exist than to exist forever
and never be a part of beauty
our attitude toward life
is come easy go easy
we are like human beings
used to be before they became
too civilized to enjoy themselves

and before i could argue him
out of his philosophy
he went and immolated himself
on a patent cigar lighter
i do not agree with him
myself i would rather have
half the happiness and twice
the longevity

but at the same time i wish
there was something i wanted
as badly as he wanted to fry himself
                              archy

a roach of the taverns

i went into a
speakeasy the other night
with some of the
boys and we were all sitting
around under one of
the tables making
merry with crumbs and
cheese and what not but
after while a strange
melancholy descended
upon the jolly crew and
one old brown veteran roach
said with a sigh well
boys eat drink and
be maudlin for
tomorrow we are dry the
shadow of the padlock
rushes toward us
like a sahara sandstorm
flinging itself at an oasis
for years myself and my
ancestors before me have
inhabited yonder ice box but
the day approaches
when our old homestead
will be taken away from
here and scalded out
yes says i soon there will
be nothing but that
eheu fugaces stuff
on every hand i
never drank it says he
what kind of a
drink is it
it is bitter as wormwood

[97]

says i and the
only chaser to it is
the lethean water
it is not the booze itself
that i regret so
much said the old brown
roach it is the
golden companionship of
the tavern myself
and my ancestors have been
chop house and tavern
roaches for hundreds of years
countless generations back
one of my elizabethan
forbears was plucked from
a can of ale in the
mermaid tavern by
will shakespeare and
put down kit marlowe s back
what subtle wits they were in
those days said i yes
he said and later
another one of my
ancestors was
introduced into a larded
hare that addison
was eating by dicky steele
my ancestor came
skurrying forth dicky
said is that your own
hare joe or a wig a
thing which addison
never forgave yours is a
remarkable family
history i said yes he
said i am the last
of a memorable
line one of my
ancestors was found drowned
in the ink well

out of which poor
eddie poe wrote the
raven we have
always associated with wits
bohemians and bon
vivants my maternal
grandmother was slain by
john masefield with
a bung starter well well it
is sad i said the
glad days pass yes
he says soon we will all
be as dry as the
egyptian scarab that
lies in the sarcophagus
beside the mummy of rameses and
he hasn t had a
drink for four thousand
years it is sad for
you he continued but
think how much sadder it
is for me with
a family tradition such as
mine only one of my
ancestors cheese it i said
interrupting him i do
not wish to injure
your feelings but i weary
of your ancestors i
have often noticed that
ancestors never boast
of the descendants who boast
of ancestors i would
rather start a family than
finish one blood will tell but often
it tells too much

                              archy

the froward lady bug

boss is it not awful
the way some female
creatures mistake ordinary
politeness for sudden
adoration
i met a katydid in a
beef stew in ann
street the other evening her
foot slipped and she
was about to sink
forever when i pushed her a
toothpick since i
rescued her the poor silly
thing follows me about
day and night i always felt
my fate would be a
poet she says to me how lovely
to be rescued by one i
am musical myself my
nature is sensitive to it so
much so that for
months i dwelt in a grand
piano in carnegie hall i
hope you don t think
i am bold no i said you
seem timid to me you
seem to lack courage entirely the
way you dog my footsteps
one would think you
were afraid to be alone i do
not wish any one any
ill luck but if
this shrinking thing got
caught in a high wind and
was blown out to

[100]

open sea i hope she would
be saved by a ship
outward bound for
madagascar

                    archy

pete the parrot and shakespeare

i got acquainted with
a parrot named pete recently
who is an interesting bird
pete says he used
to belong to the fellow
that ran the mermaid tavern
in london then i said
you must have known
shakespeare know him said pete
poor mutt i knew him well
he called me pete and i called him
bill but why do you say poor mutt
well said pete bill was a
disappointed man and was always
boring his friends about what
he might have been and done
if he only had a fair break
two or three pints of sack
and sherris and the tears
would trickle down into his
beard and his beard would get
soppy and wilt his collar
i remember one night when
bill and ben jonson and
frankie beaumont
were sopping it up

here i am ben says bill
nothing but a lousy playwright
and with anything like luck
in the breaks i might have been
a fairly decent sonnet writer
i might have been a poet
if i had kept away from the theatre

yes says ben i ve often
thought of that bill
but one consolation is
you are making pretty good money
out of the theatre

money money says bill what the hell
is money what i want is to be
a poet not a business man
these damned cheap shows
i turn out to keep the
theatre running break my heart
slap stick comedies and
blood and thunder tragedies
and melodramas say i wonder
if that boy heard you order
another bottle frankie
the only compensation is that i get
a chance now and then
to stick in a little poetry
when nobody is looking
but hells bells that isn t
what i want to do
i want to write sonnets and
songs and spenserian stanzas
and i might have done it too
if i hadn t got
into this frightful show game
business business business
grind grind grind
what a life for a man
that might have been a poet

well says frankie beaumont
why don t you cut it bill
i can t says bill
i need the money i ve got
a family to support down in

the country well says frankie
anyhow you write pretty good
plays bill any mutt can write
plays for this london public
says bill if he puts enough
murder in them what they want
is kings talking like kings
never had sense enough to talk
and stabbings and stranglings
and fat men making love
and clowns basting each
other with clubs and cheap puns
and off color allusions to all
the smut of the day oh i know
what the low brows want
and i give it to them

well says ben jonson
don t blubber into the drink
brace up like a man
and quit the rotten business
i can t i can t says bill
i ve been at it too long i ve got to
the place now where i can t
write anything else
but this cheap stuff
i m ashamed to look an honest
young sonneteer in the face
i live a hell of a life i do
the manager hands me some mouldy old
manuscript and says
bill here s a plot for you
this is the third of the month
by the tenth i want a good
script out of this that we
can start rehearsals on
not too big a cast
and not too much of your
damned poetry either

you know your old
familiar line of hokum
they eat up that falstaff stuff
of yours ring him in again
and give them a good ghost
or two and remember we gotta
have something dick burbage can get
his teeth into and be sure
and stick in a speech
somewhere the queen will take
for a personal compliment and if
you get in a line or two somewhere
about the honest english yeoman
it s always good stuff
and it s a pretty good stunt
bill to have the heavy villain
a moor or a dago or a jew
or something like that and say
i want another
comic welshman in this
but i don t need to tell
you bill you know this game
just some of your ordinary
hokum and maybe you could
kill a little kid or two a prince
or something they like
a little pathos along with
the dirt now you better see burbage
tonight and see what he wants
in that part oh says bill
to think i am
debasing my talents with junk
like that oh god what i wanted
was to be a poet
and write sonnet serials
like a gentleman should

well says i pete
bill s plays are highly

esteemed to this day
is that so says pete
poor mutt little he would
care what poor bill wanted
was to be a poet

                    archy

horse shakespeare and i

archy confesses

    coarse
    jocosity
    catches the crowd
    shakespeare
    and i
    are often
    low browed

    the fish wife
    curse
    and the laugh
    of the horse
    shakespeare
    and i
    are frequently
    coarse

aesthetic
excuses
in bill s behalf
are adduced
to refine
big bill s
coarse laugh

but bill
he would chuckle
to hear such guff
he pulled
rough stuff
and he liked
rough stuff

hoping you
are the same
      archy

mehitabel he says—

the old trouper

i ran onto mehitabel again
last evening
she is inhabiting
a decayed trunk
which lies in an alley
in greenwich village
in company with the
most villainous tom cat
i have ever seen
but there is nothing

wrong about the association
archy she told me
it is merely a plutonic
attachment
and the thing can be
believed for the tom
looks like one of pluto s demons
it is a theatre trunk
archy mehitabel told me
and tom is an old theatre cat
he has given his life
to the theatre
he claims that richard
mansfield once
kicked him out of the way
and then cried because
he had done it and
petted him
and at another time
he says in a case
of emergency
he played a bloodhound
in a production of
uncle tom s cabin
the stage is not what it
used to be tom says
he puts his front paw
on his breast and says
they don t have it any more
they don t have it here
the old troupers are gone
there s nobody can troupe
any more
they are all amateurs nowadays
they haven t got it
here
there are only
five or six of us oldtime
troupers left
this generation does not know

what stage presence is
personality is what they lack
personality
where would they get
the training my old friends
got in the stock companies
i knew mr booth very well
says tom
and a law should be passed
preventing anybody else
from ever playing
in any play he ever
played in
there was a trouper for you
i used to sit on his knee
and purr when i was
a kitten he used to tell me
how much he valued my opinion
finish is what they lack
finish
and they haven t got it
here
and again he laid his paw
on his breast
i remember mr daly very
well too
i was with mr daly s company
for several years
there was art for you
there was team work
there was direction
they knew the theatre
and they all had it
here
for two years mr daly
would not ring up the curtain
unless i was in the
prompter s box
they are amateurs nowadays
rank amateurs all of them

[111]

for two seasons i played
the dog in joseph
jefferson s rip van winkle
it is true i never came
on the stage
but he knew i was just off
and it helped him
i would like to see
one of your modern
theatre cats
act a dog so well
that it would convince
a trouper like jo jefferson
but they haven t got it
nowadays
they haven t got it
here
jo jefferson had it he had it
here
i come of a long line
of theatre cats
my grandfather
was with forrest
he had it he was a real trouper
my grandfather said
he had a voice
that used to shake
the ferryboats
on the north river
once he lost his beard
and my grandfather
dropped from the
fly gallery and landed
under his chin
and played his beard
for the rest of the act
you don t see any theatre
cats that could do that
nowadays
they haven t got it they

haven t got it
here
once i played the owl
in modjeska s production
of macbeth
i sat above the castle gate
in the murder scene
and made my yellow
eyes shine through the dusk
like an owl s eyes
modjeska was a real
trouper she knew how to pick
her support i would like
to see any of these modern
theatre cats play the owl s eyes
to modjeska s lady macbeth
but they haven t got it nowadays
they haven t got it
here

mehitabel he says
both our professions
are being ruined
by amateurs
                             archy

archy declares war

i am going to start
a revolution
i saw a kitchen
worker killing
water bugs with poison
hunting pretty
little roaches
down to death
it set my blood to
boiling
i thought of all
the massacres and slaughter
of persecuted insects
at the hands of cruel humans
and i cried
aloud to heaven
and i knelt
on all six legs
and vowed a vow
of vengeance
i shall organize the insects
i shall drill them
i shall lead them
i shall fling a billion
times a billion billion
risen insects in an army
at the throats
of all you humans
unless you sign the papers
for a damn site better treatment
volunteers volunteers
hearken to my calling
fifty million flies
are wanted may the first
to die in marmalade

curses curses curses
on the cruel human race
does not the poor mosquito
love her little offspring
that you swat against the wall
out of equatorial
swamps and fever jungles
come o mosquitoes
a billion billion strong
and sting a billion baldheads
till they butt against each other
and break like egg shells
caterpillars locusts
grasshoppers gnats
vampire moths
black legged spiders
with red hearts of hell
centipedes and scorpions
little gingery ants
come come come
come you tarantulas
with fury in your feet
bloodsuckers wriggle
out of the bayous
ticks cooties hornets
give up your pleasures
all your little trivial
sunday school picnics
this is war
in earnest
and red revolution
come in a cloud
with a sun hiding miracle
of small deadly wings
swarm stab and bite
what we want is justice
curses curses curses
over land air and water
whirl in a million
sweeping and swaying

cyclonic dances
whirl high and swoop
down on the cities
like a comet bearing death
in the loop and flick
of its tail
little little creatures
out of all your billions
make great dragons
that lie along the sky
and war with the sunset
and eat up the moon
draw all the poison
from the evil stars
and spit it on the earth
remember every planet
pivots on an atom
and so you are strong
i swear by the great
horned toad of mithridates
i swear by the vision
of whiskered old pythagoras
that i am very angry
i am mad as hell
for i have seen a soapy
kitchen mechanic
murdering my brothers
slaying little roaches
pathetic in their innocence
damn her red elbows
damn her spotted apron
damn her steamy hair
damn her dull eyes
that look like a pair
of little pickled onions
curses curses curses
i even heard her praised
for undertaking murder
on her own volition
and called the only perfect

cook in the city
come come come
come in your billions
tiny small feet
and humming little wings
crawlers and creepers
wigglers and stingers
scratchers borers slitherers
little forked tongues
man is at your mercy
one sudden gesture
and all his empires perish
rise
strike for freedom
curses on the species
that invented roach poison
curses on the stingy
beings that evolved
tight zinc covers
that you can t crawl under
for their garbage cans
come like a sandstorm
spewed from the mouth
of a great apocalyptic
desert making devil
come like the spray
sooty and fiery
snorted from the nostrils
of a sky eating ogre
let us have a little
direct action is the
sincere wish of
                    archy

the hen and the oriole

well boss did it
ever strike you that a
hen regrets it just as
much when they wring her
neck as an oriole but
nobody has any
sympathy for a hen because
she is not beautiful
while every one gets
sentimental over the
oriole and says how
shocking to kill the
lovely thing this thought
comes to my mind
because of the earnest
endeavor of a
gentleman to squash me
yesterday afternoon when i
was riding up in the
elevator if i had been a
butterfly he would have
said how did that
beautiful thing happen to
find its way into
these grimy city streets do
not harm the splendid
creature but let it
fly back to its rural
haunts again beauty always
gets the best of
it be beautiful boss
a thing of beauty is a
joy forever
be handsome boss and let

who will be clever is
the sad advice
of your ugly little friend
                    archy

ghosts

you want to know
whether i believe in ghosts
of course i do not believe in them
if you had known
as many of them as i have
you would not
believe in them either
perhaps i have been
unfortunate in my acquaintance
but the ones i have known
have been a bad lot
no one could believe in them
after being acquainted with them
a short time
it is true that i have met
them under peculiar
circumstances
that is while they
were migrating into the
bodies of what human beings
consider a lower order
of creatures
before i became a cockroach
i was a free verse poet
one of the pioneers of the artless art
and my punishment for that
was to have my soul
enter the body of a cockroach
the ghosts i have known
were the ghosts of persons
who were waiting for a vacant
body to get into
they knew they were going
to transmigrate into the bodies of
lizards lice bats snakes

worms beetles mice alley cats
turtles snails tadpoles
etcetera
and while they were waiting
they were as cross as all get out
i remember talking to one of them
who had just worked his way
upward again he had been in the
body of a flea and he was going
into a cat fish
you would think he might be
grateful for the promotion
but not he
i do not call this much of an advance
he said why could i not
be a humming bird or something
kid i told him it will
take you a million years to work your
way up to a humming bird
when i remember he said
that i used to be a hat check boy
in a hotel i could
spend a million years weeping
to think that i should come to this
we have all seen better days i said
we have all come down in the world
you have not come down as far
as some of us
if i ever get to be a hat check boy
again he said i will sting
somebody for what i have had to suffer
that remark will probably cost you
another million years among
the lower creatures i told him
transmigration is a great thing
if you do not weaken
personally my ambition is to get
my time as a cockroach shortened for
good behavior and be promoted
to a revenue officer

it is not much of a step up but
i am humble
i never ran across any of this
ectoplasm that sir arthur
conan doyle tells of but it sounds
as if it might be wonderful
stuff to mend broken furniture with

archy

archy hears from mars

at eleven o clock
p m on last saturday evening
i received the following
message on my
own private radio set
good evening little archibald
and how are you
this is mars speaking
i replied at once
whom or who
as the case may be
do i know on mars
every one here is familiar
with your work archy
was the answer
and we feel well repaid
for all the trouble we have had
in getting in touch
with your planet
thank you i replied
i would rather hear
mars say that
than any other planet
mars has always been
one of my favorite planets
it is sweet of you
to think that way about us

said mars
and so we continued to pay
each other interstellar
compliments
what is or are
thirty five million miles
between kindred souls
tell us all about
your planet said mars
well i said it is
round like an orange
or a ball
and it is all cluttered
up with automobiles
and politicians
it doesn t know where it is
going nor why
but it is in a hurry
it is in charge of a
two legged animal called
man who is genuinely
puzzled as to whether
his grandfather was a god
or a monkey
i should think said mars
that what he is himself
would make more difference
than what his grandfather was
not to this animal i replied
he is the great alibi ike of
the cosmos when he raises hell
just because he feels like
raising hell
he wants somebody to blame it on
can t anything be done about him
said mars
i am doing the best i can
i answered
but after all i am only one
and my influence is limited

you are too modest archy
said mars
we all but worship you
here on this planet
a prophet said i is not
without honor save on his own
planet wait a minute
said mars
i want to write that down
that is one of your best things
archy is it original
it was once i answered truthfully
and may be again
won t you tell us a little
something said mars
about yourself what you look like
and what you think
is the best thing you have written
and your favorite games
and that sort of thing
well i said i am brunette
and stand over six feet
without any shoes on
the best skits i have done
were some little plays
i dashed off
under the general title
of shakespeare s plays
and my favorite sport is theology
you must meet
a great many interesting people
said mars
oh yes i said one becomes
accustomed to that after a while
what is your favorite dish
said mars and do you believe
in the immortality of the soul
stew i said and yes
at least mine is immortal
but i could name several others

that i have my doubts about
is there anything else
of interest about your planet
which you wish to tell your
many admirers on mars
asked mars
there is very little else
of any real interest i said
and now will you tune out
and let me do some work
you people who say you admire
my work are always butting in
and taking up my time
how the hell can i get any
serious literary work done
if you keep bothering me
all the time now you get off
the ether and let me do some
deep thinking
you might add that i am shy
and loathe publicity
                              archy

—you gotta dance till the sun comes up . . .

mehitabel dances with boreas

well boss i saw mehitabel
last evening
she was out in the alley
dancing on the cold cobbles
while the wild december wind
blew through her frozen whiskers
and as she danced
she wailed and sang to herself
uttering the fragments
that rattled in her cold brain
in part as follows

whirl mehitabel whirl
spin mehitabel spin
thank god you re a lady still
if you have got a frozen skin

blow wind out of the north
to hell with being a pet
my left front foot is brittle
but there s life in the old dame yet

dance mehitabel dance
caper and shake a leg
what little blood is left
will fizz like wine in a keg

wind come out of the north
and pierce to the guts within
but some day mehitabel s guts
will string a violin

moon you re as cold as a frozen
skin of yellow banan
that sticks in the frost and ice
on top of a garbage can

and you throw a shadow so chilly
that it can scarcely leap
dance shadow dance
you ve got no place to sleep

whistle a tune north wind
on my hollow marrow bones
i ll dance the time with three good feet
here on the alley stones

freeze you bloody december
i never could stay a pet
but i am a lady in spite of hell
and there s life in the old dame yet

whirl mehitabel whirl
flirt your tail and spin
dance to the tune your guts will cry
when they string a violin

eight of my lives are gone
it s years since my fur was slicked
but blow north wind blow
i m damned if i am licked

girls we was all of us ladies
we was o what the hell
and once a lady always game
by crikey blood will tell

i might be somebody s pet
asleep by the fire on a rug
but me i was always romantic
i had the adventurous bug

caper mehitabel caper
leap shadow leap
you gotta dance till the sun comes up
for you got no place to sleep

i might have been many a tom cat s wife
but i got no regret
i lived my life as i liked my life
and there s pep in the old dame yet

blow wind out of the north
you cut like a piece of tin
slice my guts into fiddle strings
and we ll have a violin

spin mehitabel spin
you had a romantic past
and you re gonna cash in dancing
when you are croaked at last

i will not eat tomorrow
and i did not eat today
but wotthehell i ask you
the word is toujours gai

whirl mehitabel whirl
i once was a maltese pet
till i went and got abducted
and cripes i m a lady yet

whirl mehitabel whirl
and show your shadow how
tonight its dance with the bloody moon
tomorrow the garbage scow

whirl mehitabel whirl
spin shadow spin
the wind will pipe on your marrow bones
your slats are a mandolin

by cripes i have danced the shimmy
in rooms as warm as a dream
and gone to sleep on a cushion
with a bellyfull of cream

it s one day up and next day down
i led a romantic life
it was being abducted so many times
as spoiled me for a wife

dance mehitabel dance
till your old bones fly apart
i ain t got any regrets
for i gave my life to my art

whirl mehitabel whirl
caper my girl and grin
and pick at your guts with your frosty feet
they re the strings of a violin

girls we was all of us ladies
until we went and fell
and oncet a thoroughbred always game
i ask you wotthehell

it s last week up and this week down
and always the devil to pay
but cripes i was always the lady
and the word is toujours gai

be a tabby tame if you want
somebody s pussy and pet
the life i led was the life i liked
and there s pep in the old dame yet

whirl mehitabel whirl
leap shadow leap
you gotta dance till the sun comes up
for you got no place to sleep
                                        archy

archy at the zoo

the centipede adown the street
goes braggartly with scores of feet
a gaudy insect but not neat

the octopus s secret wish
is not to be a formal fish
he dreams that some time he may grow
another set of legs or so
and be a broadway music show

oh do not always take a chance
upon an open countenance
the hippopotamus s smile
conceals a nature full of guile

[130]

human wandering through the zoo
what do your cousins think of you

i worry not of what the sphinx
thinks or maybe thinks she thinks

i have observed a setting hen
arise from that same attitude
and cackle forth to chicks and men
some quite superfluous platitude

serious camel sad giraffe
are you afraid that if you laugh
those graceful necks will break in half

a lack of any mental outlet
dictates the young cetacean s spoutlet
he frequent blows like me and you
because there s nothing else to do

when one sees in the austral dawn
a wistful penguin perched upon
a bald man s bleak and desert dome
one knows tis yearning for its home

the quite irrational ichneumon
is such a fool it s almost human

despite the sleek shark s far flung grin
and his pretty dorsal fin
his heart is hard and black within
even within a dentist s chair
he still preserves a sinister air
a prudent dentist always fills
himself with gas before he drills
                                        archy

the dissipated hornet

well boss i had a
great example of the corrupting
influence of the great
city brought to my notice recently a
drunken hornet blew in here
the other day and sat down in the
corner and dozed and buzzed not a
real sleep you know one of those wakeful
liquor trances with the
fuzzy talk oozing out of it to hear
this guy mumble in his dreams he was right
wicked my name he says is crusty bill
i never been licked and i never will and
then he would go half way asleep
again nobody around here wanted to
fight him and after a while he got
sober enough to know how drunk he had
been and began to cry over it and get
sentimental about himself mine is a wasted
life he says but i had a good
start red liquor ruined me he says and
sobbed tell me your story i
said two years ago he said i was a country
hornet young and strong and handsome i
lived in a rusty rainspout with my
parents and brothers and sisters and all was
innocent and merry often in that happy
pastoral life would we swoop down
with joyous laughter and sting the school
children on the village green but on an evil
day alas i came to the city in a crate
of peaches i found myself in a market
near the water front alone and friendless in the
great city its ways were strange to
me food seemed inaccessible i thought

that i might starve to death as i was buzzing
down the street thinking these gloomy
thoughts i met another hornet
just outside a speak easy kid he says
you look down in the mouth forget
it kid i will show you how to live without
working how i says watch me he says just
then a drunken fly came crawling out
of the bar room in a leisurely way my new
found friend stung dissected and consumed that fly
that s the way he says smacking his lips
this is the life that was a beer fly
wait and i will get you a cocktail fly this
is the life i took up that life alas the
flies around a bar room get so drunk drinking
what is spilled that they are helpless all a
hornet has to do is wait calmly until
they come staggering out and there is his
living ready made for him at first being
young and innocent i ate only beer flies but
the curse of drink got me the mad life began
to tell upon me i got so i would not eat a
fly that was not full of some strong and heady
liquor the lights and life got me i would
not eat fruits and vegetables any more i scorned
flies from a soda fountain
they seemed flat and insipid to me
finally i got so wicked that i
went back to the country and got six innocent
young hornets and brought them back
to the city with me i started them in the
business i debauched them and
they caught my flies for me now i am in
an awful situation my six hornets from the
country have struck and set up on their own
hook i have to catch my flies myself
and my months of idleness and
dissipation have spoiled my technique i
can t catch a fly now unless he is dead drunk
what is to become of me alas the curse

[133]

of alcoholic beverages especially with each
meal well i said it is a sad story
bill and of a sort only too
common in this day of ours it is he says i
have the gout in my stinger so bad
that i scream with pain every time i spear
a fly i got into a safe place on the
inside of the typewriter and yelled out at him
my advice is suicide bill all the time
he had been pitying himself my sympathy had
been with the flies

                                        archy

unjust

poets are always asking
where do the little roses go
underneath the snow
but no one ever thinks to say
where do the little insects stay
this is because
as a general rule
roses are more handsome
than insects
beauty gets the best of it
in this world
i have heard people
say how wicked it was
to kill our feathered
friends
in order to get
their plumage and pinions
for the hats of women
and all the while
these same people
might be eating duck
as they talked
the chances are

that it is just as discouraging
to a duck to have
her head amputated
in order to become
a stuffed roast fowl
and decorate a dining table
as it is for a bird
of gayer plumage
to be bumped
off the running board of existence
to furnish plumage
for a lady s hat
but the duck
does not get the sympathy
because the duck
is not beautiful
the only insect
that succeeds in getting
mourned is a moth
or butterfly
whereas every man s
heel is raised against
the spider
and it is getting harder
and harder for spiders
to make an honest living
at that since
human beings have invented
so many ways
of killing flies
humanity will shed poems
full of tears
over the demise of
a bounding doe
or a young gazelle
but the departure of a trusty
camel leaves the
vast majorities
stonily indifferent
perhaps the theory is

that god would not have made
the camel so ugly
if the camel were not wicked
alas exclamation point
the pathos of ugliness
is only perceived
by us cockroaches of the world
and personally
i am having to stand for a lot
i am getting it double
as you might say
before my soul
migrated into the body
of a cockroach
it inhabited the carcase
of a vers libre poet
some vers libre poets are beautiful
but i was not
i had a little blond mustache
that every one thought was a mistake
and yet since i have died
i have thought of that
with regret
it hung over a mouth
that i found it difficult to keep closed
because of adenoidal trouble
but it would have been better
if i could have kept it closed
because the teeth within
were out of alignment
and were of odd sizes
this destroyed my acoustics
as you might say
my chin was nothing much
and knew it
and timidly shrank
into itself
receding from the battle of life
my eyes were all right
but my eyebrows

were scarcely noticeable
i suppose though that if
i had had noticeable eyebrows
they would have been wrong
somehow
well well not to pursue
this painful subject
to the uttermost and ultimate
wart and freckle
i was not handsome and it hampered
me when i was a human
it militated against me
as a poet
more beautiful creatures could
write verse worse than mine
and get up and recite it
with a triumphant air
and get away with it
but my sublimest ideas
were thought to be a total
loss when people saw
where they came from
i think it would have been
only justice
if i had been sent to inhabit
a butterfly
but there is very little
justice in the universe
what is the use
of being the universe
if you have to be just
interrogation point
and i suppose the universe
has so much really important
business on hand
that it finds it impossible
to look after the details
it is rushed
perhaps it has private
knowledge to the effect

that eternity is brief
after all
and it wants to get the big
jobs finished in a hurry
i find it possible to forgive
the universe
i meet it in a give and take spirit
although i do wish
that it would consult me at times
please forgive
the profundity of these
meditations
whenever i have nothing
particular to say
i find myself always
always plunging into cosmic
philosophy
or something

                 archy

the cheerful cricket

i can t see for the
life of me what there is
about crickets that makes people
call them jolly they
are the parrots of the insect race
crying cheer up cheer up
cheer up over and
over again till you want to
swat them i hate one of these
grinning skipping smirking
senseless optimists worse
than i do a cynic or a
pessimist there was
one in here the other day i was
feeling pretty well
and pleased with the world when
he started that confounded
cheer up cheer up cheer up stuff
fellow i said i am
cheerful enough or i was till
a minute ago but you
get on my nerves it s all right

to be bright and merry
but what s the use
pretending you have more
cheerfulness than there is in the
world you sound
insincere to me you insist on
it too much you make
me want to sit in
a tomb and listen to the
screech owls telling
ghost stories to the tree toads i
would rather that i heard a door squeak have
you only one record the sun
shone in my soul today before
you came and you
have made me think of the
world s woe groan
once or i will go mad your
voice floats around the world like
the ghost of a man
who laughed himself to death
listening to funny stories
the boss told i listen to you
and know why shakespeare
killed off mercutio so
early in the play it is only
hamlet that can
find material for five acts
cheer up cheer up cheer up he
says bo i told him i
wish i was the
woolworth tower i would fall
on you cheer up cheer up cheer
up he says again

                              archy

all a spook has to do is stick around

clarence the ghost

the longer i live the more i
realize that everything is
relative even morality is
relative things you would not do
sometimes you would do other
times for instance i would not consider
it honorable in me as a
righteous cockroach to crawl into a
near sighted man s soup that
man would not have a sporting chance but
with a man with ordinarily good eye
sight i should say it was
up to him to watch his soup himself and
yet if i was very tired and hungry
i would crawl into even a near
sighted man s soup knowing all the
time it was wrong and my necessity would
keep me from reproaching myself too

bitterly afterwards you can
not make any hard and fast rule
concerning the morality of crawling into
soup nor anything else a certain
alloy of expediency improves the
gold of morality and makes
it wear all the longer consider a
ghost if i were a ghost i
would not haunt ordinary people but i
would have all the fun i wanted to with
spiritualists for spiritualists are
awful nuisances to ghosts i knew a
ghost by the name of clarence one
time who hated spiritualists with a
great hatred you see said clarence they
give me no rest they have got my
number once one of those psychics gets a
ghost s number so he has to come
when he is called they work him till
the astral sweat stands out in beads
on his spectral brow they seem to think
said clarence that all a spook has to do
is to stick around waiting to dash in
with a message as to whether mrs millionbucks
pet pom has pneumonia or only wheezes
because he has been eating too many
squabs clarence was quite
bitter about it but wait he says till
the fat medium with the red nose
that has my number
passes over and i can get my
clutches on him on equal terms there s
going to be some initiation beside
the styx several of the boys are
sore on him a plump chance i have
don t i to improve myself and pass on
to another star with that medium
yanking me into somebody s parlor to
blow through one of these little tin
trumpets any time of the day or night

honest archy he says i hate the sight of a
ouija board would it be moral he
says to give that goof a bum tip on the
stock market life ain t worth
dying he says if you ve got to fag
for some chinless chump of a psychic
nor death ain t worth living
through would it be moral in me to
queer that simp with his
little circle by saying he s got an
anonymous diamond brooch in his pocket
and that his trances are rapidly developing
his kleptomania no clarence i said it
wouldn t be moral but it
might be expedient there s a ghost
around here i have been trying to get
acquainted with but he is shy i think he is
probably afraid of cockroaches

archy

she likely thinks she s nesting
on her rocky island home

some natural history

the patagonian
penguin
is a most
peculiar
bird
he lives on
pussy
willows
and his tongue
is always furred
the porcupine
of chile
sleeps his life away
and that is how
the needles
get into the hay
the argentinian
oyster
is a very
subtle gink

for when he s
being eaten
he pretends he is
a skink
when you see
a sea gull
sitting
on a bald man s dome
she likely thinks
she s nesting
on her rocky
island home
do not tease
the inmates
when strolling
through the zoo
for they have
their finer feelings
the same
as me and you
oh deride not
the camel
if grief should
make him die
his ghost will come
to haunt you
with tears
in either eye
and the spirit of
a camel
in the midnight gloom
can be so very
cheerless
as it wanders
round the room
                    archy

prudence

i do not think a prudent one
will ever aim too high
a cockroach seldom whips a dog
and seldom should he try

and should a locust take a vow
to eat a pyramid
he likely would wear out his teeth
before he ever did

i do not think the prudent one
hastes to initiate
a sequence of events which he
lacks power to terminate

for should i kick the woolworth tower
so hard i laid it low
it probably might injure me
if it fell on my toe

i do not think the prudent one
will be inclined to boast
lest circumstances unforeseen
should get him goat and ghost

for should i tell my friends i d drink
the hudson river dry
a tidal wave might come and turn
my statements to a lie

archy

this morning—

archy goes abroad

london england
since i have been
residing in westminster
abbey i have learned
a secret that i desire
to pass on to the psychic
sharps it is this
until the body of a human
being perishes utterly
the spirit is not
released from its vicinity
so long as there is any
form left in the physical
part of it the ghost can not go
to heaven or to hell
the ancient greeks
understood this and they
burned the body very often
so that the spirit could
get immediate release

the ancient egyptians
also knew it
but they reacted differently
to the knowledge
they embalmed the body
so that the form would
persist for thousands
of years and the ghost would have
to stick around for a time
here in westminster abbey
there are hundreds of
ghosts that have not yet
been released
some of them are able to wander
a few miles away
and some of them cannot
go further than a few hundred
yards from the graves
where the bodies lie
for the most part they make
the best of it
they go out on little
excursions around london
and at night they sit on
their tombs and
tell their experiences
to each other
it is perhaps the most
exclusive club in london
henry the eighth came in
about three oclock this morning
after rambling about
piccadilly for a couple of hours
and i wish i had the
space to report in detail
the ensuing conversation
between him and charles dickens
now and then
a ghost can so influence
a living person that you

might say he had grabbed off
that living person s body and was
using it as his own
edward the black prince
was telling the gang
the other evening
that he had been leading the life
of a city clerk for three weeks
one of those birds
with a top hat and a sack coat
who come floating through
the mist and drizzle
with manuscript cases
under their arms looking unreal
even when they are not animated
by ghosts edward the black prince
who is known democratically
as neddie black here
says this clerk was a mild and
humble wight when he took
him over but he worked
him up to the place where
he assaulted a policeman
saturday night then left him **flat**
one of the most pathetic
sights however
is to see the ghost of queen
victoria going out every
evening with the ghost
of a sceptre in her hand
to find mr lytton strachey
and bean him it seems she **beans**
him and beans him and he
never knows it
and every night on the stroke
of midnight elizabeth tudor
is married to walter raleigh by **that**
eminent clergyman
dr lawrence sterne
the gang pulls a good **many**

[149]

pageants which are written
by ben jonson but i think
the jinks will not be properly
planned and staged until
j m barrie gets here
this is the jolliest bunch
i have met in london
they have learned
since they passed over
that appearances and suety
pudding are not all they were
cracked up to be more anon from your little friend
archy

archy at the tomb of napoleon

paris france
i went over to
the hotel des invalides
today and gazed on
the sarcophagus of the
great napoleon
and the thought came
to me as i looked
down indeed it
is true napoleon
that the best goods
come in the smallest
packages here are
you napoleon with
your glorious course
run and here is
archy just in the
prime of his career
with his greatest
triumphs still before
him neither one of us

had a happy youth
neither one of us
was welcomed socially at
the beginning of his
career neither one of
us was considered much
to look at
and in ten thousand years from
now perhaps what you said and did
napoleon will be
confused with what
archy said and did
and perhaps the burial
place of neither will be
known napoleon looking
down upon you
i wish to ask you now
frankly as one famous
person to another
has it been worth
all the energy
that we expended all the
toil and trouble and
turmoil that it cost us
if you had your life
to live over
again bonaparte would
you pursue the star
of ambition
i tell you frankly
bonaparte that i myself
would choose the
humbler part
i would put the temptation
of greatness aside
and remain an ordinary
cockroach simple
and obscure but alas
there is a destiny that
pushes one forward

no matter how hard
one may try to resist it
i do not need to
tell you about that
bonaparte you know as
much about it as i do
yes looking at it in
the broader way neither
one of us has been to blame
for what he has done
neither for his great
successes nor his great mistakes
both of us napoleon
were impelled by some
mighty force external to
ourselves we are both to
be judged as great forces of
nature as tools in the
hand of fate rather than as
individuals who willed to
do what we have done
we must be forgiven
napoleon
you and i
when we have been
different from the common
run of creatures
i forgive you as i know
that you would forgive
me could you speak to me
and if you and i
napoleon forgive and
understand each other
what matters it if all
the world else find
things in both of us that
they find it hard
to forgive and understand
we have been
what we have been

napoleon and let them laugh that off
well after an hour or so of
meditation there i left
actually feeling that i
had been in communion
with that great spirit and
that for once in my
life i had understood and been
understood
and i went away feeling
solemn but likewise
uplifted mehitabel the
cat is missing

                    archy

mehitabel meets an affinity

paris france
mehitabel the cat
has been passing her
time in the dubious
company of
a ragged eared tom cat
with one mean
eye and the other
eye missing whom
she calls francy
he has been the hero
or the victim of
many desperate encounters
for part of his tail
has been removed
and his back has been chewed
to the spine
one can see at a glance
that he is a sneak thief
and an apache

a bandit with long
curved claws
you see his likes hanging
about the outdoor markets
here in paris waiting
their chance to sneak
a fish or a bit
of unregarded meat
or whimpering
among the chair legs at the
sidewalk cafes in the
evenings or slinking
down the gutters of
alleys in the old
quarters of the town
he has a raucous voice
much damaged by the night
air and yet there is a
sentimental wheedling
note in it as well
and yet withal he carries
his visible disgrace with
a jaunty air
when i asked mehitabel
where in the name of st denis
did you pick up that
romantic criminal
in the luxembourg gardens
she replied where
we had both gone to kill
birds he has been showing me
paris he does not
understand english but speak of
him with respect
he is like myself
an example of the truth
of the pythagorean idea
you know that in my body
which is that of a cat
there is reincarnated

the soul of cleopatra
well this cat here
was not always a cat either
he has seen better days
he tells me that once he was
a bard and lived here in paris
tell archy here
something about yourself francy
thus encouraged the
murderous looking animal spoke
and i append a
rough translation of
what he said

tame cats on a web of the persian woof
may lick their coats and purr for cream
but i am a tougher kind of goof
scheming a freer kind of scheme
daily i climb where the pigeons gleam
over the gargoyles of notre dame
robbing their nests to hear them scream
for i am a cat of the devil i am

i ll tell the world i m a hard boiled oeuf
i rend the clouds when i let off steam
to the orderly life i cry pouf pouf
it is worth far less than the bourgeois deem
my life is a dance on the edge de l abime
and i am the singer you d love to slam
who murders the midnight anonyme
for i am a cat of the devil i am

when the ribald moon leers over the roof
and the mist reeks up from the chuckling stream
i pad the quais on a silent hoof
dreaming the vagabond s ancient dream
where the piebald toms of the quartier teem
and fight for a fish or a mouldy clam
my rival i rip and his guts unseam
for i am a cat of the devil i am

roach i could rattle you rhymes by the ream
in proof of the fact that i m no spring lamb
maybe the headsman will finish the theme
for i am a cat of the devil i am
mehitabel i said
your friend is nobody else
than francois villon
and he looks it too

               archy

mehitabel sees paris

paris france
i have not been
to geneva but i have been
talking to a french cockroach
who has just returned
from there traveling all the
way in a third class
compartment he says there is no
hope for insect or man in
the league of nations
what prestige it ever had is gone
and it never had any
the idea of one great brotherhood
of men and insects on earth
is very attractive to me
but mehitabel the cat
says i am a communist an
anarchist and a socialist
she has been shocked to the soul
she says by what the
revolutionists did here during
the revolution
i am always the aristocrat archy
she said i may go and play
around montmartre and that sort
of thing and in fact i was
playing up there with francy last
night but i am always the lady
in spite of my little larks
toujours gai archy and toujours
the lady that is my motto in
spite of
ups and downs
what they did to us aristocrats
at the time of the revolution

was a plenty archy
it makes my heart bleed
to see signs of it all
over town those poor
dear duchesses that got it
in the neck i can sympathize
with them archy i may not
look it now but i come of a
royal race myself
i have come down in the world
but wotthehell archy wotthehell
jamais triste archy jamais triste
that is my motto
always the lady and always
out for a good time
francy and i lapped up
a demi of beer in a joint
up on the butte last night
that an american tourist
poured out for us
and everybody laughed and it
got to be the fashion up there
to feed beer to us cats
i did not get a vulgar souse
archy no lady gets a vulgar
souse wotthehell i hope i am above
all vulgarity but i did get a
little bit lit up
and francy did too we came
down and got on top of the
new morgue and sang and did
dances there
francy seems to see
something attractive about
morgues when he gets lit up
the old morgue he says was
a more romantic morgue but
vandal hands have torn it down
but wotthehell archy this one
will do to dance on

francy is showing me a side
paris he says tourists don t often
get a look at he has a little
love nest down in the
catacombs where
he and i are living now
he and i go down there
and do the tango amongst the
bones he is really a most
entertaining and agreeable
companion archy and he has some
very quaint ideas he is busy now
writing a poem about
us two cats filled with beer
dancing among the bones
sometimes i think francy
is a little morbid
when i see these lovely old places
that us aristocrats built archy
in the hands of the bourgeois it
makes me almost wild
but i try to bear up i try
to bear up i find agreeable
companions and put a good face
on it toujours gai that is my
motto toujours gai
francy is a little bit done up
today he tried to steal a
partridge out of a frying
pan in a joint up on the butte
we went back there for more beer
after our party
at the morgue
and the cook beaned him with
a bottle poor francy i
should hate to lose him
but something tells me i should
not stay a widow long
there is something in the air
of paris archy

[159]

that makes one young again
there s more than one
dance in the old dame yet
and with these words she
put her tail in the air and
capered off down the alley
i am afraid we shall never
get mehitabel back to america

                              archy

mehitabel in the catacombs

paris france
i would
fear greatly for the morals
of mehitabel the cat if she had any
the kind of life she
is leading is too violent
and undisciplined for words
she and the disreputable
tom cat who claims to have
been francois villon
when he was on earth
before have taken up their
permanent abode in the catacombs
whence they sally
forth nightly on excursions
of the most undignified nature
sometimes they honor
with their presence the cafes
of montparnasse and the boul mich
and sometimes they
seek diversion in the cabarets
on top of the butte
of montmartre
in these localities
it has become the fashion
among the humans

to feed beer to these
peculiar cats and they dance
and caper when they have
become well alcoholized
with this beverage
swinging their tails and
indulging in raucous feline
cries which they evidently
mistake for a song
it was my dubious
privilege to see them
when they returned to their
abode early yesterday morning
flushed as you might say
with bocks and still
in a holiday mood
the catacombs of paris are
not lined with the bones
of saints and martyrs
as are those of rome
but nevertheless these cats
should have more respect
for the relics of mortality
you may not believe me
but they actually danced and
capered among
the skeletons while the cat
who calls himself
francois villon gave forth
a chant of which the following
is a free translation

outcast bones from a thousand biers
click us a measure giddy and gleg
and caper my children dance my dears
skeleton rattle your mouldy leg
this one was a gourmet round as a keg
and that had the brow of semiramis
o fleshless forehead bald as an egg
all men s lovers come to this

this eyeless head that laughs and leers
was a chass daf once or a touareg
with golden rings in his yellow ears
skeleton rattle your mouldy leg
marot was this one or wilde or a wegg
who dropped into verses and down the abyss
and those are the bones of my old love meg
all men s lovers come to this

these bones were a ballet girl s for years
parbleu but she shook a wicked peg
and those ribs there were a noble peer s
skeleton rattle your mouldy leg
and here is a duchess that loved a yegg
with her lipless mouth that once drank bliss
down to the dreg of its ultimate dreg
all men s lovers come to this

prince if you pipe and plead and beg
you may yet be crowned with a grisly kiss
skeleton rattle your mouldy leg
all men s lovers come to this

                                        archy

off with the old love

paris france
i think
mehitabel the cat and the
outcast feline
who calls himself francois
villon are about to
quarrel and separate
mehitabel is getting tired
of living in the catacombs
she said to me
last evening
archy i sometimes wish
that francy's gaiety
did not so frequently take
a necrological turn
when francy is really happy
he always breaks
into a series of
lyric epitaphs
personally archy
i am a lady who can
be gay outside of
a mausoleum
as for morgues
and cemeteries i can
take them or i can
leave them alone
just because some of my
ancestors are now mummies
i do not feel
that i have to wait
till i see a sarcophagus
before i cheer up
i can fall in love
with a gentleman friend without

speculating how he is going
to look to the undertaker
and when i want to sing
a comic song
i do not always feel
impelled to hunt up a tomb
for a stage
i am a lady of refinement
archy i have had my ups
and downs and i have made
a few false steps in life
but i am toujours la grande dame
archy always the lady
old kid to hell with anything
coarse or unrefined
that has always been my motto
and the truth is that this
francy person has a yellow
streak of commonness
running through his poetic nature
i fell for him archy
but i feel there is trouble
coming we had words last
night over something no real
gentleman would have noticed
and the slob said to me
mehitabel if you make eyes again
at that tortoise shell
cat over there i will slice
your eyes out
with a single sweep of my claws
and toss them to the pigeons
archy those are words
that no gentleman would use
or no lady would take
you piebald fish thief
i told him
if i were not too refined
i would rip you
from the gullet to the mid riff

it is lucky for you
you frog eating four flush
that i always remember
my breeding
otherwise you would be
a candidate for what they call
civet stew in paris
something i won't stand for in a
gentleman friend
is jealousy of every other
person who may be attracted to me
by my gaiety and
aristocratic manner
and if i hear another word
out of you
i will can you first
and kill you afterwards
and then i will ignore you
archy a gentleman
with any real spirit
would have swung on me
when i said that
but this quitter let me
get away with it
i clawed him a little archy
just to show him i could
and the goof stood for it
no cat can hold me archy
that lets me claw him without
a come back i am a strong free
spirit and i live my own
life and only a masterful
cave cat can hold my affections
he must be a gentleman
but he must also make me feel
that he could be a
wild cat if he would
this francy person is neither
one nor the other
ah me archy i am afraid

[165]

my little romance
is drawing to a close
and no meal ticket in sight
either but what the hell archy
a lady can always find friends
it won't be the first time
i have been alone in the world
toujours gai archy
that is my motto
there's more than one dance
in the old dame yet

        archy

archy s life of mehitabel

the life of mehitabel the cat

boss i am engaged on a literary
work of some importance it is
nothing more nor less
than the life story of
mehitabel the cat she is
dictating it a word
at a time and all
the bunch gather around to listen but
i am rewriting it as i go along

[169]

boss i wish we
could do something
for mehitabel she is
a cat that has seen
better days she has
drunk cream at fourteen
cents the half pint
in her time and now she
is thankful for a
stray fish head from a
garbage cart but she is
cheerful under it all toujours
gai is ever her word
toujours gai kiddo drink she
says played a great
part in it all she
was taught to drink
beer by a kitchen maid she
trusted and was
abducted from a luxurious home
on one occasion in a
taxicab while under
the influence of beer which
she feels certain had been
drugged but still her
word is toujours gai my
kiddo toujours gai wotto hell
luck may change
                              archy

when along came my father bold

the minstrel and the maltese cross

well boss i promised to tell you
something of the life story of
mehitabel the cat archy says she i
was a beautiful kitten and as good
and innocent as i was beautiful my
mother was an angora you dont
look angora i said your fur
should show it did
i say angora said mehitabel it must
have been a slip of the tongue my
mother was high born and of
ancient lineage part persian and part
maltese a sort of maltese cross
i said archy she said please

do not josh my mother i
cannot permit levity in connection
with that saintly name she knew many
troubles did my mother and
died at last in a slum far from
all who had known her in her better
days but alas my father
was a villain he too had noble blood
but he had fallen into dissolute
ways and wandered the
alleys as the leader of a troupe of
strolling minstrels stealing milk
from bottles in the early mornings
catching rats here there and
everywhere and only too frequently
driven to the expedient of dining on
what might be found in
garbage cans and suburban
dump heaps now and
then a sparrow or a robin fell to my
fathers lot for he was a mighty hunter i
have heard that at times he even
ate cockroaches and as she said
that she spread
her claws and looked at me with her
head on one side i got into the works
of the typewriter mehitabel i
said try and conquer that wild and
hobohemian strain in your blood archy
she said have no fear i have dined
today but to resume my
mother the pampered beauty that she
was was eating whipped cream one
day on the back
stoop of the palace where she resided
when along came my father bold
black handsome villain that he was and
serenaded her his must have been a
magnetic personality for in spite of
her maiden modesty and

cloistered upbringing she responded
with a few well rendered musical
notes of her own i
will not dwell upon the wooing suffice
it to say that ere long they
not only sang duets together but
she was persuaded to join
him and his troupe of strollers in
their midnight meanderings alas that
first false step she
finally left her luxurious home it was
on a moonlight night in may i have
often heard her say and again and
again she has said to me that she
wished that robert w chambers could

have written her story or maybe john
galsworthy in his later and
more cosmopolitan manner well to
resume i was born in a stable in
greenwich village which was at
the time undergoing transformation
into a studio my
brothers and sisters were drowned
dearie i often look back on my life and
think how romantic it has all
been and wonder what fate saved
me and sent my brothers and sisters
to their watery grave archy i
have had a remarkable life go
on telling about it i said never
mind the side remarks i became
a pet at once continued
mehitabel but let us not make the first
instalment too long the
tale of my youth will be reserved
for your next chapter to be continued
                                    archy

we could muzzle the child

mehitabel s first mistake

well i said to
mehitabel the cat continue
the story of your life i
was a pampered kitten for
a time archy she said but
alas i soon
realized that my master and
mistress were becoming
more and more fond of a
dog that lived with
them in the studio he was
an ugly mutt take it from
me archy a red eyed little bull
dog with no manners i
hope i was too much of a lady

to show jealousy i have
been through a great deal
dearie now up and now down
but it is darn seldom
i ever forget i was a
lady always genteel archy
but this red eyed mutt was
certainly some pill and those
people were so stuck on
him that it would have made
you sick they called him
snookums and it was snookums
this and snookums that and
ribbons and bells and porterhouse
steak for him and if he
got a flea on him they called a
specialist in only one
day archy i hear my
mistress say snookums ookums
is lonely he ought to
have some one to play with
true said her husband every
dog should be brought up along
with a baby a dog
naturally likes a child to
play with we will have no
children said she a
vulgar foolish little child
might harm my snookums we
could muzzle the child said
her husband i am sure
the dog would like one to
play with and they
finally decided they would get
one from a foundling home
to play with snookums if
they could find a child
with a good enough pedigree
that wouldnt give any
germs to the dog well

[176]

one day the low lived mutt
butted in and tried to
swipe the cream i was drinking even
as a kitten archy i
never let any one put anything
across on me although i
am slow in starting
things as any real lady
should be dearie i let
this stiff snookums get
his face into the saucer
and then what i did
to his eyes and nose with
my claws would melt the
heart of a trained
nurse the simp had no
nerve he ran to his
mistress and she came after
me with a broom i
got three good scratches
through her silk stockings
archy dearie before i
was batted into the
alley and i picked myself
up out of a can full
of ashes a cat without a
home a poor little
innocent kitten alone
all alone in the great and
wicked city but i never
was one to be down
on my luck long archy my
motto has always been
toujours gai archy toujours
gai always jolly archy
always game and thank god
always the lady i
wandered a block or
two and strayed into
the family entrance of

a barroom it was my
first mistake mehitabels
adventures will be continued
archy

men shrank back from me

the curse of drink

to continue the story
of mehitabel the cat
she says to me when i
walked into that
barroom i was hungry and
mewing with despair
there were two men sitting
at the table and
looking sad i rubbed
against the legs of one
of them but he never moved
then i jumped up on
the table and stood
between them they both stared
hard at me and
then they stared at each
other but neither one
touched me or said anything

[179]

in front of one of
them was a glass full
of some liquid with
foam on the top of it i
thought it was milk
and began to drink from the
glass little did i
know archy as i lapped
it up that it was beer the
men shrank back from me and
began to tremble and shake
and look at me
finally one of them said to
the other i know what you
think bill what do i
think jeff said the
other you think bill that
i have the d ts said the
first one you think i
think i see a cat drinking
out of that beer glass but
i do not think i
see a cat at all that is all
in your imagination it
is you yourself that
have the d ts no said the
other one i dont think
you think you see a
cat i was not thinking
about cats at all i
do not know why you mention
cats for there are no
cats here just then a
salvation army lassie came
in and said you
wicked men teaching that poor
little innocent cat to
drink beer what cat
said one of the men she
thinks she sees a cat

[180]

said the other and
laughed and laughed
just then a mouse ran
across the floor and i
chased it and the salvation
lassie jumped on a
chair and screamed jeff
said bill i suppose now you
think i saw a
mouse i wish bill you
would change the
subject from animals said
jeff there is nothing
to be gained by talking
of animals mehitabel s
life story will be
continued in an early number
                    archy

a mouse ran across the floor

[181]

one day i left the place

pussy café

for some weeks said
mehitabel the cat continuing the
story of her life i
lived in that barroom and
though the society was
not what i had
been used to yet i
cannot say that it was
not interesting three
times a day in
addition to scraps from

the free lunch
and an occasional mouse
i was given a saucer
full of beer sometimes i
was given more and
when i was feeling
frolicsome it was the custom
for the patrons to gather
round and watch me
chase my tail until
i would suddenly fall
asleep at that time
they gave me the
nickname of pussy café but
one day i left the
place in the pocket
of a big fur
overcoat worn by
a gentleman who was
carrying so much that i thought
a little extra burden would
not be noticed he got
into a taxi cab
which soon afterwards
pulled up in front of
a swell residence uptown
and wandered up the
steps well said his
wife meeting him in the
hallway you are here
at last but where is my
mother whom i sent you to
the train to meet
could this be she asked
the ladys husband
pulling me out of his
coat pocket by the neck and
holding me up with a
dazed expression on his face
it could not said his

[183]

wife with a look of
scorn mehitabels life
story will be continued
before long

                archy

a communication from archy

well boss i am
sorry to report that
mehitabel the cat has
struck no more story archy
she said last night
without pay art for arts
sake is all right but
i can get real
money in the movies the
best bits are to
come too she says my life
she says has been a
romantic one boss she has
the nerve to hold out
for a pint of
cream a day i am sick
of milk she says and
why should a lady author
drink ordinary milk cream
for mine she says
and no white of egg beaten
up on top of it either i
know what my dope
is worth boss it is
my opinion she has the
swell head over getting into
print i would hate
to stop the serial
but she needs a
lesson listen archy she said
to me what i want
with my stuff is
illustrations too the next
chapter is about me taking
my first false step well

archy i either get an
illustration for that or else
i sign up with these
movie people who are always
after me you will be
wanting to sing into a phonograph
next i told her
my advice is to
can her at once i will fill
the space with my own
adventures

                    archy

rganizing the ants the worms the wasps the bees
for a revolt against mankind

the return of archy

where have i been so long
you ask me
i have been going up
and down like the devil
seeking what i might devour
i am hungry always hungry
and in the end i shall
eat everything
all the world shall come at
last to the multitudinous maws

of insects
a civilization perishes
before the tireless teeth
of little little germs
ha ha i have thrown off the mask
at last
you thought i was only
an archy
but i am more than that
i am anarchy
where have i been you ask
i have been organizing the insects
the ants the worms the wasps
the bees the cockroaches
the mosquitoes
for a revolt against mankind
i have declared war
upon humanity
i even i shall fling
the mighty atom
that splits a planet asunder
i ride the microbe
that crashes down olympus
where have i been you ask me where
i am jove and from my seat
on the edge of a bowl of beef stew
i launch the thunderous
molecule
that smites a cosmos into bits
where have i been you ask
but you had better ask
who follows in my train
there is an ant
a desert ant a tamerlane
who ate a pyramid in rage
that he might get at and devour
the mummies of six hundred
kings who in remote
antiquity had stepped upon
and crushed ascendants of his

my myrmidons
are trivial things
and they have always ruled
the world
and now they shall strike down mankind
i shall show you how
a solar system
pivots on the nubbin
of a flageolet bean
i shall show you how a blood clot
moving in a despot's brain
flung a hundred million men
to death and disease
and plunged a planet into woe
for twice a hundred years
we have the key
to the fourth dimension
for we know the little things
that swim and swarm
in protoplasm
i can show you love and hate
and the future
dreaming side by side
in a cell
in the little cells where
matter is so fine it merges
into spirit
you ask me where i have been
but you had better
ask me where i am
and what
i have been drinking
exclamation point

                      archy

archy turns highbrow for a minute

boss please let me
be highbrow for
a minute i
have just been eating
my way through some of
the books on your desk
and i have digested two of them
and it occurs to me
that antoninus the emperor
and epictetus the slave
arrived at the same
philosophy of life

[190]

that there is neither mastery
nor slavery
except as it exists
in the attitude of the soul
toward the world
thank you for listening
to a poor little
cockroach

                              archy

archy experiences a seizure

"Where have you been so long? And what on earth do
you mean by coming in here soused?" we asked Archy
as he zigzagged from the door to the desk.

He climbed onto the typewriter keys and replied in-
dignantly:

        soused yourself i havent had a drink
    and yet i am elevated i admit it i have
    been down to a second hand book
    store eating a lot of kiplings earlier
    poetry it always excites me if i eat
    a dozen stanzas of it i get all lit up
    and i try to imitate it get out of my
    way now i feel a poem in the kipling
    manner taking me

And before we could stop him he began to butt on the
keys:

    the cockroach stood by the mickle
        wood in the flush of the astral dawn

We interrupted. "Don't you mean Austral instead of
astral?"

Archy became angered and wrote peevishly:

i wrote astral and i meant astral
you let me be now i want to get this
poem off my chest you are jealous if
you were any kind of a sport at all
you would fix this machine so it could
write it in capitals it is a poem about
a fight between a cockroach and a
lot of other things get out of my way
im off

the cockroach stood by the mickle
   wood in the flush of the astral dawn
and he sniffed the air from the hidden
   lair where the khyber swordfish spawn
and the bilge and belch of the glutton
   welsh as they smelted their warlock cheese
surged to and fro where the grinding
   floe wrenched at the headlands knees
half seas over under up again
and the barnacles white in the moon
the pole stars chasing its tail like a pup again
and the dish ran away with the spoon

the waterspout came bellowing out of
   the red horizons rim
and the grey typhoon and the black
   monsoon surged forth to the
   fight with him
with three fold might they surged to
   the fight for they hated the great
   bull roach
and they cried begod as they lashed
   the sod and here is an egg to
   poach
we will bash his mug with his own raw
   lug new stripped from off his
   dome
for there is no law but teeth and claw
   to the nor nor east of nome

the punjab gull shall have his skull
    ere he goes to the burning ghaut
for there is no time for aught but crime
    where the jungle lore is taught
across the dark the afghan shark is
    whining for his head
there shall be no rule but death and
    dule till the deep red maws are
    fed
    half seas under up and down
    again
    and her keel was blown off in a
    squall
    girls we misdoubt that we ll ever
        see town again
    haul boys haul boys haul.

"Archy," we interrupted, "that haul, boys, is all right
to the eye, but the ear will surely make it hall boys.
Better change it."

        you are jealous you let me alone im off again

    the cockroach spat and he tilted his
        hat and he grinned through the
        lowering mirk
    the cockroach felt in his rangoon belt
        for his good bengali dirk
    he reefed his mast against the blast
        and he bent his mizzen free
    and he pointed the cleats of his bin
        nacle sheets at the teeth of the
        yesty sea
    he opened his mouth and he sluiced
        his drouth with his last good
        can of swipes
    begod he cried they come in pride but
        they shall go home with the
        gripes

[193]

begod he said if they want my head it
   is here on top of my chine
it shall never be said that i doffed my
   head for the boast of a heathen
   line
and he scorned to wait but he dared
   his fate and loosed his bridle rein
and leapt to close with his red fanged
   foes in the trough of the
   screaming main
from hell to nome the blow went home
   and split the firmament
from hell to nome the yellow foam
   blew wide to veil the rent
and the roaring ships they came to
   grips in the gloom of a dripping
   mist

"Archy," we interrupted again, "is there very much
more of it? It seems that you might tell in a very few
words now who won the fight, and let it go at that. Who
did win the fight, Archy?"

But Archy was peeved, and went sadly away, after
writing:

of course you wont let me finish i never saw as jealous
a person as you are

*to bring humans and cockroaches into
a better understanding*

peace—at a price

one thing the human
bean never seems to
get into it is the
fact that humans
appear just as unnecessary to
cockroaches as cockroaches
do to humans
you would scarcely
call me human
nor am i altogether

cockroach i
conceive it to be my
mission in life to bring
humans and cockroaches
into a better understanding
with each other to
establish some sort of
entente cordiale or
hands across the kitchen sink
arrangement
lately i heard a number
of cockroaches discussing
humanity one big
regal looking roach
had the floor and he spoke
as was fitting in blank verse
more or less
says he
how came this monster with the heavy
foot harsh voice and cruel heart to
rule the world
had it been dogs or cats or elephants
i could have acquiesced and found a
justice working in the decree but man
gross man
the killer man the bloody minded
crossed unsocial death dispenser of this
sphere who slays for pleasure slays
for sport for whim
who slays from habit breeds to slay and
slays
whatever breed has humors not his own
the whole apparent universe one sponge
blood filled from insect mammal fish
and bird
the which he squeezes down his vast
gullet friends i call on you to rise and
trample down this monster man this
tyrant man hear hear said
several of the wilder spirits

and it looked to me for a
minute as if they
were going right out and
wreck new york city but
an old polonius looking
roach got the floor
he cleared his throat three times
and said
what our young friend here
so eloquently counsels against
the traditional enemy is
calculated of course to appeal to
youth what he says
about man is all very true
and yet we must remember that
some of our wisest
cockroaches have always
held that there
is something impious in the
idea of overthrowing man
doubtless the supreme being
put man where he is and
doubtless he did it
for some good purpose which
it would be very
impolitic yea well nigh
blasphemous for us to enquire
into the project of
overthrowing man is indeed
tantamount to a
proposition to overthrow the
supreme being himself and
i trust that no one of
my hearers is so wild or
so wicked as to think
that possible or desirable i
cannot but admire the
idealism and patriotism of
my young friend who
has just spoken nor do i

[197]

doubt his sincerity but i
grieve to see so
many fine qualities
misdirected and i
should like to ask him
just one question to wit
namely as follows is it not
a fact that just before
coming to this meeting
he was almost killed by a
human being as he
crawled out of an ice box
and is it not true that
he was stealing food from
the said ice box and is it
not a fact that his own
recent personal experience has
as much to do with
his present rage as any
desire to better the
condition of the cockroaches of
the world in general
i think that it is the sense of
this meeting that a
resolution be passed censuring
mankind and at the
same time making it
very clear that nothing like
rebellion is to be attempted
and so on
well polonius had his way
but it is my belief that the
wilder spirits will gain the
ascendancy and if the
movement spreads to the other
insects the human race is in
danger as a friend of both
parties i should regret war
what we need is
intelligent propaganda who is

better qualified to handle
the propaganda fund than
yours truly

archy

as a friend of both parties
i should regret war

mehitabel again

well boss mehitabel the
cat is sore at me she says
that it was my fault
that you cut off her story
of her life right in
the middle and she
has been making my life a
misery to me three
times she has almost clawed
me to death i wish
she would eat a poisoned
rat but she wont she
is too lazy to catch one well
it takes all sorts of
people to make an
underworld
                              archy

archy among the philistines

i wish i had more human society
these other cockroaches here are just cockroaches
no human soul ever transmigrated into them
and any soul that would go into one of them
after giving them the once over
would be a pretty punk sort of a soul
you cant imagine how low down they are with no
esthetic sense and no imagination or anything like
that and they actually poke fun at me because I used to
be a poet before i died and my soul migrated into a
cockroach they are as crass and philistine as some
humans i could name their only thought is food but
there is a little red eyed spider lives behind your

steam radiator who has considerable sense
i don't think he is very honest though i dont know
whether he has anything human in him or is just
spider i was talking to him the other day and was
quite charmed with his conversation
after you he says pausing by the radiator
and i was about to step back of the radiator ahead
of him when something told me to watch my step
and i drew back just in time
to keep from walking into a web
there were some cockroach legs and wings
still sticking in that web
i beat it as quickly as i could up the wall
well well says that spider you are in quite a hurry archy
ha ha so you wont be at my dinner table today then
some other time cockroach some other time
i will be glad to welcome you to dinner archy
he is not to be trusted but he is the only insect
i have met for weeks that has any intelligence if you
will look back of that locker where you hang your
hat you will find a dime has rolled there i wish you
would get it and spend it for doughnuts a cent at a time
and leave the doughnuts under your typewriter i get tired
of apple peelings i nearly drowned in your ink well last
night dont forget the doughnuts

                                        archy

    We are trying to fix up some scheme whereby Archy
can use the shift keys and thus get control of the capital
letters and punctuation marks. Suggestions for a work-
able device will be thankfully received. As it is Archy has
to climb upon the frame of the typewriter and jump with
all his weight upon the keys, a key at a time, and it is only
by almost incredible exertions that he is able to drag the
paper forward so he can start a new line.

CAPITALS AT LAST

archy protests

say comma boss comma capital
i apostrophe m getting tired of
being joshed about my
punctuation period capital t followed by
he idea seems to be
that capital i apostrophe m
ignorant where punctuation
is concerned period capital n followed by
o such thing semi
colon the fact is that
the mechanical exigencies of
the case prevent my use of
all the characters on the

typewriter keyboard period
capital i apostrophe m
doing the best capital
i can under difficulties semi colon
and capital i apostrophe m
grieved at the unkindness
of the criticism period please
consider that my name
is signed in small
caps period

                    archy period

CAPITALS AT LAST

I THOUGHT THAT SOME HISTORIC DAY
SHIFT KEYS WOULD LOCK IN SUCH A WAY
THAT MY POETIC FEET WOULD FALL
UPON EACH CLICKING CAPITAL
AND NOW FROM KEY TO KEY I CLIMB
TO WRITE MY GRATITUDE IN RHYME
YOU LITTLE KNOW WITH WHAT DELIGHT
THROUGHOUT THE LONG AND LONELY
   NIGHT
I'VE KICKED AND BUTTED (FOOT AND BEAN)
AGAINST THE KEYS OF YOUR MACHINE
TO TELL THE MOVING TALE OF ALL
THAT TO A COCKROACH MAY BEFALL
INDEED IF I COULD NOT HAVE HAD
SUCH OCCUPATION I'D BE MAD
AH FOR A SOUL LIKE MINE TO DWELL
WITHIN A COCKROACH THAT IS HELL
TO SCURRY FROM THE PLAYFUL CAT
TO DODGE THE INSECT EATING RAT
THE HUNGRY SPIDER TO EVADE
THE MOUSE THAT %)?))" " " $$$((gee boss
what a jolt that cat mehitabel made
a jump for me
i got away but she unlocked the shift key

it kicked me right into the
mechanism where she
couldn't reach me it
was nearly the death of little
archy that kick spurned me right
out of parnassus back into
the vers libre slums i lay
in behind the wires for an hour after
she left before i dared to get
out and finish i hate
cats say boss please lock the shift
key tight some night
i would like to tell the story of
my life all in capital
letters

arch·

the stuff of literature

_nank your friends for me for
all their good advice about how to
work your typewriter but what i have
always claimed is that manners and methods
are no great matter compared
with thoughts in poetry you cant hide
gems of thought so they wont flash
on the world on the other hand if you press
agent poor stuff that wont make it live
my ego will express itself in spite of
all mechanical obstacles having something
to say is the thing being sincere
counts for more than forms of expression thanks
for the doughnuts

archy

a meal for every goat

archy s autobiography

if all the verse what I have wrote
were boiled together in a kettle
twould make a meal for every goat
from nome to popocatapetl
mexico

and all the prose what I have penned
if laid together end to end
would reach from russia to south bend
indiana

but all the money what I saved
from all them works at which i slaved

is not enough to get me shaved
every morning

and all the dams which i care
if heaped together in the air
would not reach much of anywhere
they wouldnt

because i dont shave every day
and i write for arts sake anyway
and always hate to take my pay
i loathe it

and all of you who credit that
could sit down on an opera hat
and never crush the darn thing flat
you skeptics

                                    archy

quote and only man is vile quote

as a representative
of the insect world
i have often wondered
on what man bases his claims
to superiority
everything he knows he has had
to learn whereas we insects are born
knowing everything we need to know
for instance man had to invent
airplanes before he could fly
but if a fly cannot fly
as soon as he is hatched
his parents kick him out and disown him
i should describe the human race
as a strange species of bipeds
who cannot run fast enough
to collect the money

which they owe themselves
as far as government is concerned
men after thousands of years practice
are not as well organized socially
as the average ant hill or beehive
they cannot build dwellings
as beautiful as a spiders web
and i never saw a city
full of men manage to be as happy
as a congregation of mosquitoes
who have discovered a fat man
on a camping trip
as far as personal beauty
is concerned who ever saw
man woman or child
who could compete with a butterfly
if you tell a dancer
that she is a firefly
she is complimented
a musical composer
is all puffed up with pride
if he can catch the spirit
of a summer night full of crickets
man cannot even make war
with the efficiency and generalship
of an army of warrior ants
and he has done little else
but make war for centuries
make war and wonder
how he is going to pay for it
man is a queer looking gink
who uses what brains he has
to get himself into trouble with
and then blames it on the fates
the only invention man ever made
which we insects do not have
is money and he gives up
everything else to get money
and then discovers that it is not worth
what he gave up to get it

in his envy he invents
insect exterminators
but in time every city he builds
is eaten down by insects
what i ask you is babylon now
it is the habitation of fleas
also nineveh and tyre
humanitys culture consists
in sitting down in circles
and passing the word around
about how darned smart humanity is
i wish you would tell
the furnace man at your house
to put out some new brand
of roach paste i do not get
any kick any more out of the brand
he has been using the last year
formerly it pepped me up
and stimulated me
i have a strange tale about
mehitabel to tell you
more anon

archy

investigating her morals

mehitabel s morals

boss i got
a message from
mehitabel the cat
the other day
brought me by
a cockroach
she asks for our help
it seems she is being
held at ellis
island while an
investigation is made
of her morals
she left the country

and now it looks as
if she might not
be able to get
back in again
she cannot see
why they are
investigating
her morals she says
wotthehellbill she says
i never claimed
i had any morals
she has always regarded
morals as an unnecessary
complication in life
her theory is
that they take up room that might
better be devoted to
something more interesting
live while you are alive
she says and postpone
morality to the hereafter
everything in its place
is my rule she says
but i am liberal she
says i do not give
a damn how moral other
people are i never try
to interfere with them
in fact i prefer them
moral they furnish
a background for my
vivacity in the meantime
it looks as if she
would have to swim
if she gets ashore and
the water is cold

                    archy

cream de la cream

well boss mehitabel the cat
has turned up again after a long
absence she declines
to explain her movements but she
drops out dark hints of a
most melodramatic nature ups and downs
archy she says always ups and downs
that is what my life has

been one day lapping
up the cream de la cream and the
next skirmishing for
fish heads in an alley but
toujours gai archy toujours gai no
matter how the luck broke i have had a
most romantic life archy talk
about reincarnation and transmigration
archy why i could tell you things of who
i used to be archy that would make
your eyes stick out like a snails one
incarnation queening it with a tarara on
my bean as cleopatra archy and
the next being abducted as a poor
working girl but toujours gai archy toujours
gai and finally my soul has migrated to
the body of a cat and not even a persian or
a maltese at that but where have you been
lately mehitabel i asked her never mind
archy she says dont ask no questions
and i will tell no lies all i
got to say to keep away
from the movies have you been in the
movies mehitabel i asked her never mind
archy she says never mind all i got to
say is keep away from those
movie camps theres some mighty
nice people and animals connected with them
and then again theres some that aint i
say nothing against anybody archy i am
used to ups and downs no matter
how luck breaks its toujours gai
with me all i got to say
archy is that sometimes a cat
comes along that is a perfect gentleman and
then again some of the slickest furred ones
aint if i was a cat that was the
particular pet of a movie star archy and
slept on a silk cushion and had
white chinese rats especially

imported for my meals i would try to live
up to all that luxury and be a
gentleman in word and deed mehitabel i said
have you had another unfortunate romance i am
making no complaint against any
one archy she says wottell archy wottell even
if the breaks is bad my motto is toujours gai
but to slip out nights and sing and frolic
under the moon with a lady and then cut her
dead in the day time before your rich
friends and see her batted out of a studio
with a broom without raising a paw for her
aint what i call being a
gentleman archy and i am
a lady archy and i know a gentleman when
i meet one but wottell archy wottell toujours
gai is the word never say die
archy its the cheerful heart that wins all i
got to say is that if i ever get that
fluffy haired slob down on the
water front when some of my gang
is around he will wish he had
watched his step i aint vindictive archy i
dont hold grudges no lady does but i
got friends archy that maybe would take it
up for me theres a black cat with one ear
sliced off lives down around old slip is a
good pal of mine i wouldnt want to
see trouble start archy no real lady
wants a fight to start over her but
sometimes she cant hold her friends back
all i got to say is that boob with his silver
bells around his neck better sidestep old slip
well archy lets not talk any more about my troubles
does the boss ever leave any pieces of sandwich
in the waste paper basket any more honest
archy i would will myself to a furrier for a
pair of oysters i could even she says eat you
archy she said it like a joke but there
was a kind of a pondering look in her eyes

[213]

so i just crawled into the inside of
your typewriter behind the wires it
seemed safer let her hustle for a
mouse if she is as hungry as all that
but i am afraid she never will she
is too romantic to work

                                    archy

do not pity mehitabel

do not pity
mehitabel
she is having
her own kind of
a good time
in her own way
she would not
understand any other
sort of life
but the life
she has chosen
to lead
she was predestined
to it as the
sparks fly upward
chacun au son gout
as they say in france
start her in
as a kitten
and she would
repeat the same story
and do not overlook
the fact that
mehitabel is really
proud of herself
she enjoys
her own sufferings
            archy

are you abducting me percy

mehitabel tries companionate marriage

boss i have seen mehitabel the cat
again and she has just been through
another matrimonial experience
she said in part as follows
i am always the sap archy
always the good natured simp
always believing in the good intentions
of those deceitful tom cats
always getting married at leisure
and repenting in haste

[215]

its wrong for an artist to marry
a free spirit has gotta
live her own life
about three months ago along came a
maltese tom with a black heart and
silver bells on his neck and says
mehitabel be mine
are you abducting me percy i asks him
no said he i am offering marriage
honorable up to date
companionate marriage
listen i said if its marriage
theres a catch in it somewheres
ive been married again and again
and its been my experience
that any kind of marriage
means just one dam kitten after another
and domesticity always ruins my art
but this companionate marriage says he
is all assets and no liabilities
its something new mehitabel
be mine mehitabel and i promise
a life of open ice boxes
creamed fish and catnip
well i said wotthehell kid
if its something new i will take a
chance theres a dance or two
in the old dame yet
i will try any kind of marriage once
you look like a gentleman to me percy
well archy i was wrong as usual
i wont go into details for i aint
any tabloid newspaper
but the way it worked out was i rustled
grub for that low lived bum for two
months and when the kittens came
he left me flat and he says these
offsprings dissolves the wedding
i am always the lady archy
i didn t do anything vulgar

[216]

i removed his left eye with one claw
and i says to him if i wasn t an
aristocrat id rip you
from gehenna to duodenum
the next four flusher that
says marriage to me
i may really lose my temper
trial marriage or companionate
marriage or old fashioned american
plan three meals a day marriage
with no thursdays off
they are all the same thing
marriage is marriage
and you cant laugh that curse off
                                        archy

no social stuff for mehitabel

i said to mehitabel
the cat i suppose you are
going to the swell cat
show i am not archy
said she i have as
much lineage as any
of those society
cats but i never could
see the conventional
social stuff archy
i am a lady
but i am bohemian
too archy i
live my own life
no bells and pink
ribbons for me
archy it is me for
the life romantic i could
walk right into
that cat show and get

away with it
archy none of those
maltese princesses has
anything on me in the
way of hauteur
or birth either or any
of the aristocratic
fixings and condiments
that mark the
cats of lady clara
vere de vere but
it bores me archy
me for the
wide open spaces the
alley serenade and
the moonlight
sonata on the back
fences i would
rather kill my own
rats and share
them with a
friend from greenwich
village than lap up
cream or beef juice
from a silver porringer
and have to
be polite to the
bourgeois clans
that feed me
wot the hell i
feel superior to that
stupid bunch me
for a dance
across the roofs when
the red star
calls to my blood
none of your
pretty puss stuff for
mehitabel it would
give me a grouch

to have to be so
solemn toujours
gai archy toujours
gai is my
motto

                archy

a cow who has the gift of milking herself

the open spaces are too open

> boss i saw mehitabel
> the cat yesterday she is
> back in town after
> spending a couple
> of weeks
> in the country
> archy she says to me
> i will never leave the
> city again no
> matter what the weather
> may be me for the
> cobble stones and the
> asphalt and the friendly

alleys the great open
spaces are all right but
they are too open i have been
living on a diet of
open spaces the country is
all right if you have a trained
human family to rustle
up the eats for you or know
a cow who has the
gift of milking herself for
your benefit but archy
i am a city lady
i was never educated to dig for
field mice and as for calling
birds out of the trees i dont
have the musical
education for it i cant
even imitate a cat bird
i will take my chance
hereafter with the garbage
cans in town until
such times as i decorate
a rubbish heap myself
that may not be long archy
but wot the hell
i have had a good time while
i lasted come easy go easy
archy that is my motto
i tried to snatch a bone
from a terrier a month
ago and the beast bit my front
paw nearly off
but wot the hell archy
wot the hell i can still
dance a merry step or two
on three legs i am
slightly disabled archy but
still in the ring and still
i have the class wot the
hell archy i am always

a lady and always gay
and i got one eye out of
that terrier at that
i would be afraid that
mehitabel s end is not far off
if she had not been looking
as bad as she does for
at least three years
she says it is her
romantic disposition
that keeps her young
and yet i think if some
cheerful musical family
in good circumstances were to
offer mehitabel a home
where she would be treated in
all ways as one of the family
she has reached the point where
she might consent to give up
living her own life
only three legs archy she says
to me only three legs left
but wot the hell archy
there s a dance in the old
dame yet

                              archy

THEY TASTE ALIKE TO ME.

THEY DO, HEH?

random thoughts by archy

one thing that
shows that
insects are
superior to men
is the fact that
insects run their
affairs without
political campaigns
elections and so forth

  *   *   *

a man thinks
he amounts to a lot

[223]

but to a mosquito
a man is
merely
something to eat

*   *   *

i have noticed
that when
chickens quit
quarrelling over their
food they often
find that there is
enough for all of them
i wonder if
it might not
be the same way
with the
human race

*   *   *

germs are very
objectionable to men
but a germ
thinks of a man
as only the swamp
in which
he has to live

*   *   *

a louse i
used to know
told me that
millionaires and
bums tasted
about alike
to him

*   *   *

the trouble with
most people is
that they

[224]

lose their sense of
proportion
of what use is
it for a
queen bee to fall in
love with a bull

*   *   *

what is all this mystery
about the sphinx
that has troubled so many
illustrious men
no doubt the very same
thoughts she thinks
are thought every day
by some obscure hen
                    archy

archy s song

man eats the big fish
the big fish eat the
little fish
the little fish
eat insects
in the water
the water insects
eat the water plants
the water plants
eat mud
mud eats man
my favorite poem
is the same as
abraham lincolns
o why should the spirit
of mortal be proud
awaiting your answer
i am and so forth
                    archy

[225]

the waiter plucked me out

archy turns revolutionist

if all the bugs
in all the worlds
twixt earth and betelgoose
should sharpen up
their little stings
and turn their feelings loose
they soon would show
all human beans
in saturn
earth
or mars
their relative significance
among the spinning stars
man is so proud
the haughty simp
so hard for to approach

and he looks down
with such an air
on spider
midge
or roach
the supercilious silliness
of this poor wingless bird
is cosmically comical
and stellarly absurd
his scutellated occiput
has holes somewhere inside
and there no doubt
two pints or so
of scrambled brains reside
if all the bugs
of all the stars
should sting him on the dome
they might pierce through
that osseous rind
and find the brains at home
and in the convolutions lay
an egg with fancies fraught
which
germinating rapidly
might turn into a thought
might turn into the thought
that men
and insects are the same
both transient flecks
of starry dust
that out of nothing came
the planets are
what atoms are
and neither more nor less
man s feet have grown
so big that he
forgets his littleness
the things he thinks
are only things
that insects always knew

[227]

the things he does
are stunts that we
don t have to think to do
he spent a score
of centuries
in getting feeble wings
which we instinctively
acquired
with other trivial things
the day is coming
very soon
when man and all his race
must cast their silly
pride aside
and take the second place
i ll take the bugs
of all the stars
and tell them of my plan
and fling them with
their myriad stings
against the tyrant man
dear boss this outburst
is the result
of a personal insult
as so much verse always is
maybe you know how
that is yourself
i dropped into an irish
stew in a restaurant
the other evening
for a warm bath and a bite
to eat and a low browed
waiter plucked me out
and said to me
if you must eat i will
lead you to the
food i have especially prepared
for you and he took me
to the kitchen
and tried to make me

fill myself with
a poisonous concoction
known cynically as roach food
can you wonder
that my anger
against the whole human
race has blazed forth in
song when the revolution
comes i shall
do my best to save
you you have so many
points that are far
from being human

                              archy

archy s last name

boss i just discovered what
my last name is i
pass it on to you i belong to the
family of the blattidae right o
said mehitabel the cat when i told her
about it they have
got you sized up right you blatt out
everything you hear
i gleaned the information from
a bulletin issued by the
united states department of
agriculture which you left on the
floor by your desk it was entitled
cockroaches and written by
e l marlatt entomologist and acting
chief in the absence of the chief and he
tells a dozen ways of killing roaches boss
what business has the united states
government got
to sick a high salaried
expert onto a poor little roach

please leave me some
more cheerful literature also please
get your typewriter fixed the keys are
working hard again butting them as i
do one at a time with
my head i get awful pains in my
neck writing for you

archy

quote buns by great men quote

one of the most
pathetic things i
have seen recently
was an intoxicated person
trying to fall
down a moving stairway
it was the escalator at
the thirty fourth street
side of the
pennsylvania station
he could not fall down as
fast as it
carried him up again but
he was game he kept on
trying he was
stubborn about it
evidently it was a part of
his tradition habit and
training always to fall down
stairs when intoxicated and
he did not intend to
be defeated this time i
watched him for an hour
and moved sadly away thinking
how much sorrow
drink is responsible for the
buns by great men

reached and kept
are not attained
by sudden flight but they
while their companions slept
were falling upwards
through the night

                              archy

an awful warning

dear boss i was walking along
the curbstone yesterday
and i ran spang into an old bum
who was sitting happily
in the gutter singing
in part as follows

oh i ruined my prospects
by wicked desires
which i put into action
as far as i could
but now i ve arrived
within sight of hell fires
and i wish i d done better
i wish i d been good

as i sit in the gutter
and look at the sky
the man in the moon
is a looking at me
and i thinks to myself
i d have risen that high
if i had behaved myself
proper as he

now all you young fellows
and pretty young janes
as passes me by
and dont pitch me a dime

take warning by me
and avoid all the pains
which comes from remorse
in the fullness of time

and all you young fellows
thats out on a bust
and lively young flappers
so spic and so span
i oncet had a sweetheart
and me she did trust
to maintain myself always
a proper young man

i was lured to a barroom
and there i was tempted
for the bartender cried
be a man and drink rum
and after that first
glass of liquor i emptied
i found myself jobless
and went on the bum

now all you young fellows
and flappers so gay
that passes me by
and dont toss me a cent
there oncet was a time
when i went on my way
with ladylike janes
like an elegant gent

now i sits in the gutter
and looks at the stars
and wish i had always
behaved and been good
and never drunk rum
at them elegant bars
and never been wicked
as much as i could

you gents and your girl friends
should tip an old man
for his horrid example
of not being good
you must try and behave
in so far as you can
you should toss me a dime
for my warning you should
                                archy

may emulate the tumble bug

as it looks to archy

ants go on their cheerful way
merrily from day to day
building cities out of sand
and they seem to understand
dwelling therein peacefully
disciplined and orderly
and the much lauded bee contrives
for to fill his thundering hives
with a ranked society
based on work and honesty

[234]

and a thousand neat examples
could i cite of insect lives
free from much that tears and tramples
human beings and their wives
even the coral in the ocean
throughout his dim and damp existence
scorns political commotion
and labors with a glad persistence
worthy of large commendations
to erect his naval stations

man the universal simp
follows lagging with a limp
treading on his neighbors toes
the way the little insect goes
in a million years or more
man may learn the simple lore
of how the bees are organized
and why the ants are civilized
may even hope for to approach
the culture of an average roach
if he is humble and not smug
may emulate the tumble bug

for we insects now inherit
all humanity has builded
all they raised with brawn and spirit
all the domes and spires they gilded
time the anthropophagous
swallows down all human works
through his broad esophagus
moslems christians hindus turks
pass to their sarcophagus
leaving nothing much on earth
which even beetles find of worth
i mention nineveh and tyre
i cite the tower of babel
troy which fell into the fire
and sodom with its rabble
where are all the towns of siddim

where the kings of crete
long long since the desert hid em
and the spiders bite their feet
following an old convention
dating back to jeremiah
i might even mention
babylon i might enquire
where o where is babylon
and the echo answers where
for its former ruling wizards
sleep in sand and silicon
with gravel in their gizzards
and sand burrs in their hair
and the centipedes are dancing
in the chambers of the palace
where the kings and queens entrancing
used to quaff the ruby chalice
and proceed to their romancing

i look forward to the day
when the human race is done
and we insects romp and play
freely underneath the sun
and no roach paste is scattered
about anywhere i got another jolt of it
last night and today i seem to have a case
of intestinal flu the trouble with you
human beings is you are just plain wicked
                                    archy

*one of our prominent scientists
got a good look at it*

archy on the radio

dear boss
i hope you tuned in
last evening when mars and i
were on the radio together
our first joint appearance
in several years

do you realize said mars
that next week will be archy week
all over mars
and several other prominent planets

archy
good gracious mars it had slipped
my memory

mars
do you know that you are
our favorite author here and
we all but worship you

archy
well mars as far as that goes
you are one of my favorite planets

mars
what a coincidence

archy
the long arm of coincidence
makes many radio connections

mars
is that your own phrase archy

archy
mine until the next air program
nowadays an author owns his stuff
only between air programs

mars
did you know about the archy clubs here

archy
i hope they can t throw them this far
what do they look like

mars
like dumbbells ha ha ha
but please tell us how you happened
to start your career as a writer

archy
it did not happen it was something
i planned deliberately so i could quit
being what i was

mars
explain please the stars are listening

archy
well you see i was the four marx brothers
and it became annoying because
i quarrelled among myself all the time
so in order to end it all i turned
author writing dante s inferno and
mehitabel the cat

mars
what do you call that little planet
where you are at

archy
well now what do you call it

mars
we call it goofus

archy
goofus goofus why goofus

mars
not long ago one of our prominent
scientists got a good look at it
with a new fangled telescope and
he laughed himself to death crying out
goofus goofus goofus all the time
he said from the way it looked it couldn t
be named anything else but goofus

archy
well if that s the way you feel who was
that lady i seen you walking with last sunday

mars
that wasn t no lady that was venus
is there any particular message
you would like to send your billions
and billions of admirers in these parts

archy
oh yes tell them
this hour is by the courtesy
of the knockem cold roach and bug killing company
and that i wish to testify
that their product has several times
brought me personally nearer the great adventure
than any other roach paste i ever ate
i always carry a flask of bath tub gin with me
as an antidote

mars
will you describe yourself for your
worshipers here

archy
i am over six feet and go everywhere

mars
who has influenced you most in a
literary way

archy
theodore dreiser and bernard shaw
they taught me how far an author can go
if he never loses patience with himself

mars
archy it is impossible that you should
not lose patience with yourself sometimes

archy
well i havent gone as far as they have either

mars
what are the conditions of life on your planet archy

                    archy
they practically dont exist any more

                    mars
but how do people get along

                    archy
the men make a living by talking
about how much they have lost
during the depression
and the women and children pick up
what they can by listening
how is it by yourself old timer

                    mars
we never had to do any work here
we get our living by biting electrons out of the air
which we crack with our teeth
and eat the kernels while we spit
the shells into space which accounts
for a lot of the static you hear

                    archy
that not only interests me as a scientist
but it seems much more refined than
working for a living

                    mars
yes it is refined all right but it is
expensive it runs into terrible dentists bills

                    archy
but dentists bills are always terrible
everywhere anyhow

                    mars
wait till i write that down please
do you have to think a long time
for those brilliant things
or do they just come to you

                    [241]

archy

i never think at all when i write
nobody can do two things at the same time
and do them both well

mars

are you starting any new literary movements on your
planet

archy

oh yes the latest literary movement
consists in going to all the fences
and coal sheds near all the school houses
and copying off of them all the bad words
written there by naughty little boys
over the week ends
and these form the bases of the new novels
of course these novels are kept away
from the young so they will not be contaminated

mars

but where do the boys get the words

archy

from hired hands and the classics

archy

i am in fact becoming a low brow

archy a low brow

boss i saw a picture
of myself in a paper
the other day
writing on a typewriter
with some of my feet
i wish it was as easy
as that what i have to do
is dive at each key
on the machine
and bump it with my head
and sometimes it telescopes

[243]

my occiput into my
vertebrae and i have a
permanent callous
on my forehead
i am in fact becoming
a low brow think of it
me with all my learning
to become a low brow
hoping that you
will remain the same
i am as ever your
faithful little bug

                              archy

mehitabel s parlor story

boss did you
hear about the two drunks
who were riding in
a ford or something
equally comic
and the ford or
whatever it was nearly
went off the
road one of
the drunks poked the
other and said thickly
they always talk thickly in
these stories
anyway he said hey look
out how youre driving
youll have us in
the ditch in a minute if
you dont look out
why said the second
drunk who was drunker
i thought you
were driving i got

that from mehitabel the
cat its the first parlor
story ive ever heard
her tell and ive known
her for five or six
years now
                    archy

archy s mission

well boss i am
going to quit living
a life of leisure
i have been an idler
and a waster and a
mere poet too long
my conscience has waked up
wish yours would do the same
i am going to have
a moral purpose in my life
hereafter and a cause
i am going to reclaim
cockroaches and teach them
proper ways of living
i am going to see if i cannot
reform insects in general
i have constituted
myself a missionary
extraordinary
and minister
plenipotentiary
and entomological
to bring idealism to
the little struggling brothers
the conditions in the insect
world today would shock
american reformers
if they knew about them

the lives they lead
are scarcely fit to print
i cannot go into
details but the contented
laxness in which i find
them is frightful
a family newspaper is no place
for these revelations
but i am trying to have
printed in paris
for limited circulation
amongst truly earnest
souls a volume which will
be entitled
the truth about the insects
i assure you there is nothing
even in the old testament
as terrible
i shall be the cotton mather
of the boll weevil

                    archy

you can fry fish on the sidewalk

archy visits washington

washington d c july
23 well boss here
i am in washington
watching my step for fear
some one will push me
into the food bill up
to date i am the only thing
in this country that
has not been added to it by
the time this is
published nothing that
i have said may be
true however which is a

thing that is constantly happening
to thousands of
great journalists now in
washington it is so hot here that
i get stuck in the asphalt
every day on my
way from the senate press
gallery back to
shoemakers where the
affairs of the nation
are habitually settled by
the old settlers it
is so hot that you can
fry fish on the
sidewalk in any part of
town and many people
are here with fish to fry
including now
and then a german
carp i am lodging on
top of the washington
monument where i can
overlook things
you cant keep a good bug
from the top of
the column all the time i
am taking my meals with
the specimens in the
smithsonian institution when i
see any one coming i hold
my breath and look like another
specimen but in the
capitol building there
is no attention paid to me
because there are so
many other insects
around it gives you a
great idea of the
american people when you
see some of the

things they elect after july
27 address me care
st elizabeth hospital
for the insane i am going out
there for a visit with
some of your other
contributors

archy

ballade of the under side

by archy
the roach that scurries
skips and runs
may read far more than those
that fly
i know what family skeletons
within your closets
swing and dry
not that i ever
play the spy
but as in corners
dim i bide
i can t dodge knowledge
though i try
i see things from
the under side

the lordly ones the
haughty ones
with supercilious
heads held high
the up stage stiff
pretentious guns
miss much that meets
my humbler eye
not that i meddle
perk or pry

but i m too small
to feel great pride
and as the pompous world
goes by
i see things from
the under side

above me wheel
the stars and suns
but humans shut
me from the sky
you see their eyes as pure
as nuns
i see their wayward
feet and sly
i own and own it with
a sigh
my point of view
is somewhat wried
i am a pessimistic
guy
i see things from the
under side

l envoi
prince ere you pull a bluff
and lie
before you fake
and play the snide
consider whether
archy s nigh
i see things from
the under side

archy wants to end it all

well boss from time
to time i just simply
get bored with having
to be a cockroach my
soul my real ego if
you get what i mean is
tired of being shut
up in an insects body the
best you can say for it is that it
is unusual and you could
say as much for mumps so
while feeling gloomy the
other night the thought came
to me why not
go on to the next stage as
soon as possible why not
commit suicide and
maybe be reincarnated in
some higher form of life why
not be the captain of my
soul the master of my fate and
the more i pondered over it the
more i was attracted to
the notion well boss you would
be surprised to find
out how hard it is for a
cockroach to commit suicide unless
you have been one
and tried it of course i
could let mehitabel the
cat damage me and die that
way but all my finer sensibilities
revolt at the idea i jumped out
the fourth story window and
a wind caught me and blew

me into the eighth story i
tried to hang myself with a
thread and i am so light i
just swung back and forth and
didnt even choke myself shooting
is out of the question and poison
is not within
my reach i might drown myself
in the ink well but if
you ever got a mouthful of it you
would know it was a
thing no refined person could go
on with boss i am going to
end it all before long and i
want to go easy have you
any suggestion yours
for transmigration

                                archy

book review

boss a new book
has appeared
which should be
read by every one
it is entitled
the cockroach
its life history
and how to deal
with it and
the author
is frederick laing
who is assistant
in the department
of entomology in the
british museum
of natural history
it is one of the
best books i ever
tasted i am eating
the binding from
a copy with
a great deal of
relish and
recommend it
to all other
insects yours
truly
                    archy

he used to be a pet of charlemagne

archy and the old un

one of the saddest
creatures i ever saw
was a turtle who said
he was a thousand
years old
no turtle looks very
joyous the style of
architecture peculiar
to the faces and necks of
turtles is such

that even if they were to
feel gay internally
they would find difficulty
in expressing their joy
a kind of melancholy dwells
in the wrinkles of a
turtles neck the only thing
that looks sadder than a turtle
is the little dead fish
that is served in an italian
tabledhote restaurant
well this turtle i am telling you
about was so old that
he used to be a pet
of charlemagne
and he finally committed suicide
he stood on his hind
legs and jumped up
and bit himself on the
forehead and held on until
he died
i wrote a poem
about this turtle
after his death
which goes as follows

why did he die perhaps he knew
too much about
the ways of men and turtles
he had seen too much no doubt

optimist in youth of course
youth never quails
he preached to all his brother turtles
moral turtles turn to whales

but the weary ages passed
and he perceived
turtles still continued turtles
then he doubted disbelieved

brooding for two hundred years
in discontent
he became a snapping turtle
savage cynic in his bent

timon of the turtle tribe
so he withdrew
from the world remarking often
piffle there is nothing true

nothing changes all the salt
that used to be
scattered widely through the ocean
still gives flavor to the sea

nothing changes all the bunk
of long ago
still is swallowed by the nations
progress always stubs its toe

the moral well the morals quite
an easy one
do not live to be a thousand
youll be sorry ere youre done

the only way boss
to keep hope in the world
is to keep changing its
population frequently
i am sorry to be so
pessimistic today
but you see i need a change
very badly
when do we start
for hollywood
i am eager to be gone
i wish to cheer myself
up in some fashion
your faithful little
cockroach
        archibald

archygrams

the wood louse sits on a splinter
and sings to the rising sap
aint it awful how winter
lingers in springtimes lap

*   *   *

it is a good
thing not to be too
aristocratic
the oldest and
most pedigreed
families in this
country are the
occupants of various sarcophagi
in the museums
but it is dull associating
with mummies no
matter how royal their
blood used to be when
they had blood
it is like living in
philadelphia

*   *   *

honesty is a good
thing but
it is not profitable to
its possessor
unless it is
kept under control
if you are not
honest at all
everybody hates you
and if you are

[257]

absolutely honest
you get martyred.

          *   *   ❖

as i was crawling
through the holes in
a swiss cheese
the other
day it occurred to
me to wonder
what a swiss cheese
would think if
a swiss cheese
could think and after
cogitating for some
time i said to myself
if a swiss cheese
could think
it would think that
a swiss cheese
was the most important
thing in the world
just as everything that
can think at all
does think about itself

          *   *   *

these anarchists that
are going to
destroy organized
society and civilization
and everything remind
me of an ant i
knew one time
he was a big red ant a
regular bull of an
ant and he came bulging down a
garden path and ran
into a stone gate post curses on
you said the ant to the

[258]

stone gate post get out of my
way but the stone never budged
i will kick you over
said the ant and he kicked but
it only hurt his hind legs
well then said
the ant i will eat you down and
he began taking little bites
in a great rage maybe i said
you will do it in
time but it will
spoil your digestion first

         *   *   *

a good many
failures are happy
because they don t
realize it many a
cockroach believes
himself as beautiful
as a butterfly
have a heart o have
a heart and
let them dream on

         *   *   *

boss i believe
that the
millennium will
get here some day
but i could
compile quite a list
of persons
who will have
to go
first

         *   *   *

tis very seldom i have felt
drawn to a scallop or a smelt

[259]

and still more rarely do i feel
love for the sleek electric eel

             *   *   *

the oyster is useful in his fashion
but has little pride or passion

             *   *   *

when the proud ibexes start from sleep
in the early alpine morns
at once from crag to crag they leap
alighting on their horns
and may a dozen times rebound
ere resting haughty on the ground
i do not like their trivial pride
nor think them truly dignified

             *   *   *

did you ever
notice that when
a politician
does get an idea
he usually
gets it all wrong

archy says

one queer thing about
spring gardens is
that so many people
use them to
raise spinach in
instead of food

             *   *   *

everybody has two kinds of friends
one kind tries to run
his affairs for him

and the other kind
well i will be darned if i can remember
the other kind

*   *   *

now and then
there is a person born
who is so unlucky
that he runs into accidents
which started out to happen
to somebody else

*   *   *

what kind of angels are they out there

sings of los angeles

boss i see by
the papers there
has been more than
one unconventional
episode
in the far west
and i have made
a little song
as follows

los angeles
los angeles
the home of the movie star
what kind of angels
are they
out there where you are
los angeles
los angeles
much must be left
untold
but science says
that freuds rush in
where angels
fear to tread
los angeles
los angeles
clean up your
movie game
or else o city of angels
you better
change your name
yours for all the morality
that the traffic
will bear

      archy

wants to go in the movies

boss i wish you would
make arrangements to put me
into the movies a
lot of people who are no
handsomer in the face than i
am are drawing millions of
dollars a year i
have always felt that i
could act if i
were given the chance and a

truly refined cockroach might
be a novelty but do not pay
any attention to the
wishes of mehitabel the cat along
this line mehitabel
told me the other day that several
firms were bidding against
each other for her
services i would be the greatest
feline vamp in the
history of the screen said
mehitabel wot the hell archy
wot the hell ain t i a
reincarnation of cleopatra and
dont the vamp stuff come quite
natural to me i will say it
does but i have refused all
offers archy up to
date they must pay me
my price the
truth is that mehitabel hasnt a
chance and she is not a
steady character by the way
here is a piece of political news
for you mehitabel tells me that
the cats in greenwich
village and the adjoining
neighborhoods are forming soviets now
they are going in for bolshevism
her soviet she says
meets in washington mews
they are for the nationalization
of all fish markets

                                        archy

140 degrees

the retreat from hollywood

Archy, the Free Verse Cockroach, and Mehitabel the Cat, are on their way back from Hollywood, hitch-hiking. Mehitabel was forcibly ejected at least twice from every moving-picture studio in Hollywood, and nourishes animosity against the art of the cinema. Archy reports that when they left Hollywood Mehitabel and seven platinum-blonde kittens, who were attempting to follow her across the desert . . . but here is the latest bulletin from Archy:

> mehitabels third kitten succumbed
> to a scorpion today

poor little thing she said
i suppose the next one will perish
in a sandstorm and the next one
fall into the colorado river
it breaks my heart i am all
maternal instinct next to my art
as a modern dancer mother love is
the strongest thing in me
it is so strong that sometimes life seems to me
to be just one damned kitten
after another
but of course if i get back to broadway
without any kittens i will have more
freedom for my art
and can live my own life again
then she began to practice
dance steps among the cactus
casting fond eyes at a coyote

boss i am afraid
that mehitabels morals are no better
than before she struck hollywood
after all she remarked kittens
are but passing episodes in the life
of a great artist i may have been
given the bums rush from six auto camps
in three days but hells bells
i am still a lady

the loss of that kitten is a terrible grief
but an aristocrat and an artist
must bear up toujours gai
is my motto toujours gai

theres life in the old dame yet
and with that she cut a caper with
the heat at one hundred and forty
degrees fahrenheit

in new mexico where she is gadding about

artists shouldnt have offspring

A bulletin from Archy the Cockroach, who started out last July to hitch-hike from Hollywood to New York with Mehitabel the Cat and Mehitabel's seven platinum-blonde kittens:

> had a great break boss
> got a ride on the running board of a car
> and caught up with mehitabel
> in new mexico where she is gadding about
> with a coyote friend
> i asked her where the kittens were
> kittens said mehitabel kittens
> with a puzzled look on her face
> why goodness gracious i seem to remember
> that i did have some kittens
> i hope nothing terrible has happened

to the poor little things but if something has
i suppose they are better off
an artist like me shouldnt really
have offspring it handicaps her career
archy i want you to meet my boy friend
cowboy bill the coyote i call him
i am trying to get him to come to new york
with me and do a burlesque turn
isnt he handsome i said tactfully that he looked
very distinguished to me and all bill said
was nerts insect nerts

                                                archy

could such things be

A bulletin from Archy, who, with Mehitabel the Cat, started
out last July to hitch-hike from Hollywood to New York:

well boss here i am back in new york
i got a great break
after walking for months through arizona
i caught a ride on an airplane
and the first person i saw here was mehitabel
who had bummed her way
in a tourist trailer
she is living in shinbone alley
on second hand fish heads she drags away
from the east side markets
and she has some new kittens
they are the most peculiar kittens i ever saw
not the ones she left hollywood with
months ago or anything like them
there are five of these new ones
and they dont mew
they make a noise more like barking
i thought of that coyote she was so friendly with
in the southwest but i did not ask
any tactless questions
boss do you suppose such things could be
                                                archy

trying to get milk

what does a trouper care

A bulletin from Archy, who started weeks ago hitch-hiking
.cross the country from California to New York, accompanied
by Mehitabel and the seven platinum-blonde kittens she acquired in Hollywood:

> still somewhere in arizona
> sometime in october
> sand storm struck us yesterday
> i peeped out from under a rock
> and saw mehitabel dancing
> and singing as follows
> ive got a rock in my eye
> and a scorpion in my gizzard
> but what does an artist care

[269]

for a bit of red hot blizzard
my feet are full of cactus
there are blisters in my hair
but howl storm howl
what does a trouper care
i got a thirst like a mummy
i got a desert chill
but cheerio my deario
theres a dance in the old dame still
two more of the kittens disappeared
well i got three left said mehitabel
poor little dears i am afraid
they will never reach broadway
unless they learn how to get milk
from the cactus plants damn them
their appetites are spoiling my figure
a lot of encouragement a dancer gets
from her family i must say
any other artist i know would tell them
to go wean themselves on alkali
and be done with them but my great weakness
is my maternal instinct
boss i made nearly a mile today
before the sand storm blew me back
i hear texas is a thousand miles across

                                        archy

be damned mother dear

Mehitabel the Cat is still living in Shinbone Alley with the
strange kittens which arrived shortly after Mehitabel's arrival
from the Southwest. Archy, the Cockroach, says . . . but let
him tell it:

one of mehitabels kittens
licked a bull pup yesterday
and she is very proud
but hang them she says
i cant teach them to fight like cats

i told one of them yesterday
when i left home
i might bring him back
a pretty neck ribbon
if he was a good kitten
and he answered me in a strange voice
ribbon be damned mother dear
what i want is a brass collar
with spikes on it
and another one whom i had been
calling pussy says to me
pussy be damned mother dear
call me fido and another one
who got hold of a ball of catnip
complained it made him
sick at the stomach he says
catnip be damned mother dear
what i want is a bone to gnaw
what do you suppose makes them
act so strange archy
do you suppose i answered her
that prenatal influence
could have anything to do with it
perhaps that is it
she replied innocently
i seem to remember
that i was chased through
arizona and new mexico
by a coyote or did i dream it
i will say you were chased
i told her my advice
is to rent them out
to a dog and pony show

                          archy

the artist always pays

boss i visited mehitabel last night
at her home in shinbone alley
she sat on a heap of frozen refuse
with those strange new kittens she has
frolicking around her
and sang a little song at the cold moon
which went like this

i have had my ups i have had my downs
i never was nobodys pet
i got a limp in my left hind leg
but theres life in the old dame yet

my first boy friend was a maltese tom
quite handsomely constructed
i trusted him but the first thing i knew
i was practically abducted

then i took up with a persian prince
a cat by no means plain
and that exotic son of a gun
abducted me again

what chance has an innocent kitten got
with the background of a lady
when feline blighters betray her trust
in ways lowlifed and shady

my next boy friend was a yellow bum
who loafed down by the docks
i rustled that gonifs rats for him
and he paid me with hard knocks

i have had my ups i have had my downs
i have led a helluva life
it was all these abductions unsettled my **mind**
for being somebodys wife

today i am here tomorrow flung
on a scow bound down the bay
but wotthehell o wotthehell
i m a lady thats toujours gai

my next boy friend was a theater cat
a kind of a backstage pet
he taught me to dance and get me right
theres a dance in the old dame yet

my next boy friend he left me flat
with a family and no milk
and i says to him as i lifted his eye
i ll learn ye how to bilk

i have had my ups i have had my downs
i have been through the mill
but in spite of a hundred abductions kid
i am a lady still

my next friend wore a ribbon and bells
but he laughed and left me broke
and i said as i sliced him into scraps
laugh off this little joke

some day my guts will be fiddle strings
but my ghost will dance while they play
for they cant take the pep from the old girls soul
and i am toujours gai

my heart has been broken a thousand times
i have had my downs and ups
but the queerest thing ever happened to me
is these kittens as turned out pups

o wotthehell o toujours gai
i never had time to fret
i danced to whatever tune was played
and theres life in the old dame yet

i have had my ups i have had my downs
i have been through the mill
but i said when i clawed that coyotes face
thank god i am a lady still

and then she added looking at those
extraordinary kittens of hers
archy i wish you would
take a little trip up to the zoo
and see if they have any department there
for odd sizes and new species

i got to find a home
for these damned freaks somewhere
poor little things my heart bleeds for them
it agonizes my maternal instinct
one way or another an artist always pays
                                        archy

yours for rum crime and riot archy

a word from little archibald

thank you
for the mittens
socks and
muffler for me
knitted out of
frogs hair by one
of my admirers which
you so kindly
forwarded i suppose
the reason
i got them was that
they were too

small for you
to wear yourself
yours for rum
crime and riot
                archy

archy does his part

the kings of babylon are covered with fleas

prophecies

the papers are full of the prophecies
of preachers professors and laymen
to the effect that this human civilization
is on the way out
and it looks to an insect such as i
very possible
the only thing i wonder about
is why the human species calls it a civilization
human society has never been
as well organized as a hill of ants

[279]

or a hive of bees
and all the ancient sites of civilization
are now in the possession of insects
who are far superior in organization
and in their ethical practices
spiders bite the mummified feet
of the pharaohs of egypt
and the kings of babylon are covered with fleas
which they are too defunct to feel

                    archy the cockroach

repeal

we have had repeal for some months now
and a lot of devoted patriots
have been trying with all their might
to drink the country back into prosperity
and it may have made some improvement
but i have the feeling that something else
will have to be done as well
i am ashamed to say that i dont
feel any surer of what it is
that has to be done
than the economists and financiers
and other experts and wizards who are
at the present moment not doing it
but i do have the feeling that if the people
of the whole world were let alone
and there were no trade restrictions of any sort
or artificial barriers
put between them by their governments
they would speedily find the answer

                    archy the cockroach

the ballyhoo

every time a european dictator
gets at the end of his string
and cant think of any other ballyhoo
to attract the attention of the people
he begins another attack on the jews
centuries of persecution
have so hardened and sharpened the jew
that he survives his persecutors
and outsteps them and outthinks them
if these guys were smart
they would give the jews a chance
to disintegrate through luxury and ease
instead of which they toughen
the hebraic moral fibre
through the ages and they will wind up
by making the jews in the end
what they were said to be
that is the chosen people
                    archy the cockroach

the league

if the league of nations
can survive the mutual animosities
of the powers which belong to it
it is safe from the activities
of the countries which stayed outside of it
it furnishes a wonderful mechanism
with which to do what the powers
want to do if they only knew
what they wanted to do
incidentally i wonder why europe of today
is always referred to by highbrow writers

as post war europe
they seem to think that the war
which started in nineteen fourteen
is over with whereas there have been
merely a few brief truces
that war is merely worrying through
its first half century
and will only cease permanently
when a generation comes along
which has forgotten all the old feuds
                    archy the cockroach

conferences

diplomatists and ambassadors
are rushing hither and yon
from country to country around the world
by train steamer and airplane
by which i judge that there is more trouble
in store for the human species
for i have noticed that conferences
to establish international good will
always break up with another row
there is no hope for the world
unless politicians of all sorts
are completely abolished
you cannot get a millennium by
laying a whole lot of five year plans
end to end if governments would just let people alon
things would straighten out of themselves
in the course of time
                    archy the cockroach

a warning

i am glad to see business
picking up again but when i hear
that the stock market is on the rise
there is a bit of a chill
creeps over my flush of optimism
for i can remember way back
millions of years back
to the days when the stock market
was up in the stratosphere
in a wild balloon
and it came down without a parachute
if it does that all over again
we will reach a situation
where the hard times of the last few years
will look so good by comparison
that they will resemble
an ice cream party on the pastors lawn
                    archy the cockroach

now look at it

the human race never would
take my advice
and now just look at it
planning more wars which mean
more debts more trouble and still more wars
well if it wants to commit suicide
why should a little insect such as i
worry about it
a suicide is a person who has
considered his own case and decided
that he is worthless and who acts
as his own judge jury and executioner

and he probably knows better
than anyone else whether there is justice
in the verdict
i am sorry to see the human race go
for it was in some respects almost as interesting
as several species of insects
but if it wants to die off
i shall not worry about it
i shall merely conclude it knows what it wants
                              archy the cockroach

why the earth is round

the men of science are talking
about the size and shape of the universe again
i thought i had settled that for them
years ago it is as big as you think it is
and it is spherical in shape
can you prove it isnt
it is round like a ball or an orange
providence made it that shape
so it would roll when he kicked it
and if you ask me how i know this
the answer is that that is just what
i would do myself
if there are any other practical
scientific questions you would like
to have answered just write to
                              archy the cockroach

the big bad wolf

i went to a movie show
the other evening in the cuff
of a friends turned up trousers
and saw the three little pigs
and was greatly edified by the moral lesson
how cruel i said to myself
was the big bad wolf
how superior to wolves are men
the wolf would have eaten those pigs raw
and even alive
whereas a man would have kindly
cut their throats
and lovingly made them into
country sausage spare ribs and pigs knuckles
he would tenderly have roasted them
fried them and boiled them
cooked them feelingly with charity
towards all and malice towards none
and piously eaten them served with sauerkraut
and other trimmings
it is no wonder that the edible animals
are afraid of wolves and love men so
when a pig is eaten by a wolf
he realizes that something is wrong with the world
but when he is eaten by a man
he must thank god fervently
that he is being useful to a superior being
it must be the same way
with a colored man who is being lynched
he must be grateful that he is being lynched
in a land of freedom and liberty
and not in any of the old world countries
of darkness and oppression
where men are still the victims
of kings iniquity and constipation

[285]

we ought all to be grateful in this country
that our wall street robber barons
and crooked international bankers
are such highly respectable citizens
and do so much for the churches
and for charity
and support such noble institutions and foundations
for the welfare of mankind
and are such spiritually minded philanthropists
it would be horrid to be robbed
by the wrong kind of people
if i were a man i would not let
a cannibal eat me unless he showed me
a letter certifying to his character
from the pastor of his church
even our industrial murderers
in this country are usually affiliated
with political parties devoted
to the uplift
the enlightenment and the progress
of humankind
every time i get discouraged
and contemplate suicide
by impersonating a raisin and getting devoured
as part of a piece of pie
i think of our national blessings
and cheer up again
it is indeed
as i have been reading lately
a great period in which to be alive
and it is a cheering thought to think
that god is on the side of the best digestion
your moral little friend
                              archy the cockroach

abolish bridge

the administration ought to get wise
to one thing about the hard times
and recovery from them
the country was getting along all right
until everybody in it
took up contract bridge in a big way
a few years ago
everybody stopped work and did nothing
but play bridge
and the country hit the chutes
they dont know they are loafing
because there is just enough mental effort
connected with bridge so they can kid themselves
they are busy all the time
and smart and clever as the dickens
when the bridge fever subsides
the country will automatically recover itself
                                    archy the cockroach

small talk

i went into the flea circus
on broadway the other day
and heard a lot of fleas
talking and bragging to each other
one flea had been over to the swell dog show
and was boasting that he had bit
a high priced thoroughbred dog
yeah says another flea
that is nothing to get so proud of
a thoroughbred dog tastes just like a mongrel
i should think you would be more democratic
than to brag about that

go and get a reputation
said a third flea
i went into a circus last spring and bit a lion
i completely conquered him
i made him whine and cringe
he did not bite me back
get out of my way
i am the flea that licked a lion
i said to myself probably
that lion didnt even know he had been bitten
some insects are just like human beings
small talk i said to myself
and went away from there
                              archy the cockroach

the south pole

it seems admiral byrd has to discove
the south pole all over again
every little while
that comes of not discovering it
hard enough the first time
so it would stay discovered
we insects are superior to you men
in many ways
it would never have occurred to us
that the south pole cared whether it was
discovered or not
the thing that amuses me
is that the country is so busted
that a lot of people have no jobs
or food or clothes or shelter
but there is money enough to keep on
discovering the south pole
over and over again
                              archy the cockroach

poets

the universe and archy
the inspired cockroach
sat and looked at each other
satirically

you write so many things
about me that are not true
complained the universe

there are so many things
about you which you seem to be
unconscious of yourself said archy

i contain a number of things
which i am trying to forget
rejoined the universe

such as what asked archy

such as cockroaches and poets
replied the universe

you are wrong contended archy
for it is only by working up
the most important part of yourself
into the form of poets
that you get a product capable
of understanding you at all

you poets were always able
to get the better of me
in argument said the universe
and i think that is one thing
that is the matter with you

if you object to my intellect
retorted archy i can only reply
that i got it from you
as well as everything else
that should make you more humble

the two dollars

we insects have the advantage
of the human race in some respects
we dont have to worry all the time
about what a dollar is
and how to get one
i understand from my human friends
that there are two kinds of dollars
being discussed now
one kind would be worth so little
that you couldnt buy anything with it
the other kind would be worth so much
that you couldnt get hold of it
to buy anything with
i talked it over with mehitabel the cat
and she said wotthehell archy
i dont need money myself
as long as i got gentlemen friends
who blow me to meals
mehitabel has no morals
but i like her disposition
                    archy the cockroach

for reform

dear boss i am
beginning the new year
by lining myself up
with the reformers
and diplomats
cockroaches have always
been fearless
and direct in their
methods defiantly
leaping into the arena
but diplomacy is my
watchword beginning with today
i see that to put
things over i must bore
beneath like the diplomats
and camouflage my autocratic
leanings by singing
loudly about reform
and censorship which brings
me to mehitabel
she wants to break into
the movies i pointed out to her
that will hays might
object to her morals
as she has advertised them
on numerous occasions
to be rather unconventional
wotthehell archy
says mehitabel
aint i reformed now
i see that the best
way to boost mehitabel
may be to denounce her
now and then yours
for diplomacy and reform
                  archy

a horrid notion

dear boss i am hoping
and praying for the depression
to pass i was in a newspaper
office yesterday eating some nice paste
and i heard the rod and gun editor
saying to his assistant
if times dont get better before long
gentlemen anglers will have to give up
fancy bait and use cockroaches
to catch fish with
please nip this horrid notion
in the bud write at once
to the fish and game commission

                                        archy

archy in washington

Archy, the Famous Cockroach, surveys Washington—and
finds the experts running around in circles surveying each
other. Here are his views on Money, Radicals, Crop Control,
and Whatnot.

I sent Archy down to Washington recently to make
a Survey. Everyone else is making Surveys, and they
puzzle me a good deal because I can't understand them.
But Archy always uses words which I can comprehend,
and I am inclined to trust his judgment on financial, industrial and economic problems. For he has no ax to
grind.

Archy returned a little puzzled himself, and his
report to me falls naturally into the form of Question
and Answer.

QUESTION—Well, Archy, what did you learn?

ANSWER—the first thing i found was a lot of other experts making surveys the government is spending a good deal of time in surveying itself and in surveying the people who are surveying it out in lafayette park survey experts are running around in circles surveying each other

Q.—What about national finances?

A.—i discovered that there are two kinds of dollars being planned dollar number one is to be worth so little that no one can buy anything with it everybody will have it dollar number two will be worth so much that nobody can get hold of one to buy anything with nobody will have it

Q.—How about the industrial and economic situation, generally speaking?

A.—well if you mean how are you going to get rich i can tell you that in a nutshell

Q.—In a what?

A.—you know what i said and i dont want to hear any cheap wisecracks from you

here is how you may get rich

you borrow enough money from one of the government agencies to buy 100,000 acres of land

then you go and tell the government that you are going to plant 100,000 acres of wheat

then the government pays you not to plant it for if all that wheat were raised it would mean more overproduction

then you take the profits from the wheat you did not raise and buy another 100,000 acres of land

this time you tell the government that you are going to plant 100,000 acres of cotton and the government pays you not to

and so on and on it is an endless chain and will result in making everybody wealthy

Q.—But suppose the government will not pay you not to plant it?

A.—then you plant it and that puts the government in

[293]

an embarrassing position they have to pay you to destroy it after it has been planted

Q.—Where is the government going to get the money
to pay everyone for not producing anything?

A.—they are getting it from the dentists

Q.—But where do the dentists get it?

A.—out of the teeth of the public i saw hundreds of
thousands of dentists in washington

lanes of them miles long were filing into the basement
of the treasury department handing over to the government the gold they had dug out of the teeth of the
people

Q.—But are not people going to object to this after
while?

A.—not at all it hooks up with the policy of not producing foodstuffs if people are not going to get foodstuffs to eat they have no use for their teeth and the
government might just as well have them

Q.—In a general way, how is the recovery program
working out?

A.—swell but it is about time we had a program for
recovering from the recovery

Q.—What do you think of the danger of a revolution?

A.—so many people think we have already had one that
there is little danger of them trying to start it

besides how are you going to revolt against a government when you cant find out what kind of a government
it is

suppose you were a radical and started a revolution
you would feel pretty cheap wouldnt you if you found
out later that what you had revolted against was just
what you had been advocating

the thing that is going to save the country is the
fact that no one knows what is the matter with it

after while there will be a general agreement that
maybe there isnt anything much the matter with it

Q.—Archy, are you a conservative or a radical?

A.—here dont you ask me that

i got worried almost to the point of insanity asking
myself that when i was down in washington

finally i decided to end it all   i climbed to the top of
the washington monument and jumped off to commit
suicide   but i dont weigh so much   i floated to the
ground as gently as a snowflake

hell i said whats the use

fate is against me i cant even kill myself

but there are a lot of other experts who are heavier
than i am in every sense of the word

and there is the washington monument

they might have better luck and it might prove one
of the most popular features of the recovery program
Q.—Did you gain any inkling of the way to abolish
industrial troubles?
A.—oh yes that is easy

just abolish industry and there will be no further
industrial troubles
Q.—Did you survey Congress?
A.—i didnt like to run any risk of waking it up
Q.—What was your general feeling, after your in-
vestigations?
A.—optimistic   decidedly so   i think what human beings have agreed to call civilization is on its way out not
only in this country but all over the world

whatever succeeds it cant be worse and may be
better

*so many americans had been coming
to their state*

hold everything

agreements to scrap
naval vessels are what you make them
but if this country
and great britain dont want a war
theyd better cut out
international yacht races

while we are reforming
so many other things
it might not be a bad idea

to begin investigating
the efficiency displayed on passenger
ships
before they burn up or sink
instead of afterward
but of course a simple thing like that
couldnt be done by human beings
it is only ants spiders bees and other
insects
who know how to organize a society
and make it work

i have observed
a queer cycle in human affairs
a boy comes to the city
from the country
when he is twenty years old
and works his nerves into tattered
dishrags
for forty years
just to get money enough
so that he can go and live
in the country again and nurse
his nervous breakdown

i went into a flea circus
on broadway the other day
and overheard a conversation between
two of the performers
human beings said one of the clowns
never seem to understand
that they look just as funny to us fleas
as us fleas look to human beings
dont talk to me
said the ringmaster flea
about human beings
what the hell are they
except something to eat

i do not kick against my fate
i think that life is swell

contentedly i sit and wait
for the world to go to hell
and if by some queer accident
it goes the other way
i ll try and face that strange event
gamely day by day
although privately i dont think
its going anywhere in particular
its just running around in circles
chasing its tail like one
of mehitabel s fool kittens

mehitabel the cat
says she is not scared
by the cleanup in the moving pictures
cheer up says mehitabel
television is coming some time
and who knows but what television
will be lousy and enjoyable
and by the time television is
cleaned up
the pictures will get immoral
again
there is always hope says
mehitabel
if you dont weaken
the artistic purpose
of these periods of reform is
to give
greater zest to the relaxation
which follows

prince gets jail term
says a headline
selfish aristocrat
as if us communists did not need
all the jail room we can get
with a hard winter coming on
and here and there a job
looming up that has to be dodged

new england womens clubs were excited
over a questionnaire
addressed to college girls asking them
if they were interested
in a companion without marriage
or a companion with marriage
a marriage with children
or children without marriage
hells bells said mehitabel the cat
i should think they would be
interested in all of them
though perhaps not at the same time

i am continually shocked and reshocked
at the flaunting depravity of that
careless cat
and yet i suppose she serves a purpose
if there were not always someone
who needed reform and regeneration
the world would get as dull
for us good people
as two honeymoons full
of honeymoon bridge

the country is getting so full
of poor relations
that many persons are purchasing
cars with two rumble seats

i heard two bums
talking yesterday
i am afraid said the first one
that this depression will peter out
before long and we will have
to go to work
cheer up said the second one
we have weathered many
spells
of good times before this
i would almost welcome good

times again
people are so sour nowadays
and the relief agencies are
getting so critical
scab retorted his companion
quitter
the season is approaching
when there will be a lot of
big dinners
to consider what should be
done
about the hungry multitudes

when i was in hollywood
i ran across the ingenious theory
that the japs might make trouble
just because so many
americans had been coming in
to their state of california
                    archy

archy broadcasts

Announcer:
Archy the Cosmic Cockroach will now talk to you on world affairs. Archy, what do you consider the most feasible remedy for overproduction?

archy
well i dont want to go into details with a couple of million people unless i can watch their faces and make a quick change if i seem to be going too far but i will say that in my opinion the problem of overproduction has been very competently handled by the birth control productions

Announcer:
Do you think the time is ripe for launching a third national political party in America?

archy
it is more than ripe it is rotten

Announcer:
Will you give your interpretation of the Japanese activities of the past few months?

archy
all i feel free to say is that i would never pick a cherry blossom unless i were sure it did not have a wasp hidden in it

Announcer:
What changes do you suggest in our national financial system?

archy
well boss when i have money i dont want any change and when i am busted i always think oh whats the use

Announcer:
Do you think this country ought to join the League
of Nations?

archy
aint they both got trouble enough living in sin without marrying each other

Announcer:
Do you think a general adoption of the Marxian
philosophy is necessary to save the world?

archy
i always liked harpo and groucho but i never could see
karl

Announcer:
Have you any notions on farm relief?

archy
you let the farmers alone they make business for the
manufacturers when i hitch hiked from los angeles to
new york last summer i saw three thousand miles of
tractors and farm machinery sitting out in the rain
getting rusty wherever there was rain and i said to myself that is the right idea that will make money for the
manufacturers as far as the farmers are concerned they
are used to getting along without money anyhow
    all they got to do is mortgage some more land to get
new farm machinery to work the land they have just
mortgaged and that is a good deal easier than dragging
the farm machinery in under a shed   if they organized
with state or national associations to have an effect on
the prices of their product that would be a great deal
of trouble also and it might take away the chance of raising hell with their congressmen which is one of the
delights of their life
    government control of agriculture may be all right
but i should hate to see it run into agricultural control

of government because the agriculturists have never yet shown that they could control their own business let alone the business of everybody else

all they got to do is gang up efficiently among themselves to run their business but they never can stay ganged up they run out on each other

and then after they have run out on each other and caused a crop program to fail they blame somebody else for the failure

i am a great believer in letting every industry run its own affairs if it cannot learn it must perish

the farmers have the greatest natural economic leverage in the world in human necessity for their products and their failure to utilize it is not a recommendation for extending their political power

you let the farmers alone if they had rather revert to the status of peasants than progress to the status of business men that is their own business

let the railroads alone too if they can no longer compete with motor traffic without special privilege to help them let them pass and let motor traffic have its day

archy

on the air again

Archy the Cockroach made another radio "appearance" last evening; and a brief résumé of the broadcast is appended:

Announcer:

This program comes to you through the courtesy of the Knockemorf Insect Exterminator Company, Inc. . . . Ladies and gentlemen, and all you wee tots who are listening in, this is the Roach Paste Hour, and it is my privilege to introduce Archy the Cockroach on Current Events.

Archy, tell us what you think of Current Events.

archy
well with regard to currants i have never been much
of a bug for currants
i could always take them or leave them alone but with
razzberries it is different i am a bug for razzberries and
with regard to the events of the day i regard them as
beginning continuing and ending with just one fruity
razzberry after another

Announcer:
What is your program for debt settlement?

archy
my policy with regard to debts is a kind of a yes and
no policy like every other statesmans
yes it would be awfully nice if they were paid
but no they are not going to be

Announcer:
What do you think of inflation?

archy
anything you blow up ought to have a squeaker in
it so when deflation comes people will listen to the
squeaker and not realize the wind is coming out of the
situation
maybe we could get senator bilboa for the squeaker

Announcer:
Have you thought deeply concerning technocracy?

archy
oh yes indeed very deeply

Announcer:
Will you tell the listeners-in of the Roach Paste Hour
the results of your thought?

archy
i have thought too deeply for that i have thought so
far down into the subject that i am way below the place

where there could be any results and even if there were results it would take me years to climb up again far enough to announce them and by that time everything will be different

Announcer:
What do you think with regard to the tax situation in general?

archy
if i put it on the air they would not be able to use the air any more afterward

the post office department would cut out the air as a means of communication

and if i printed it in a paper it would be the last issue of that paper

if i were to use any sincere language with regard to taxes i would not be generally understood because there are only a few people in the world low life enough to understand the language i would use and they do not pay taxes

that is what i think about taxes

Announcer:
I do not quite understand you.

archy
what i mean is that most people are too decent and too well brought up to comprehend my vocabulary if i got onto the subject of taxes

Announcer:
What do you think about Wall Street?

archy
i think nature will take its course if we leave things alone

i was down that way one day last fall and i noticed at one end of wall street was a river and at the other end was a cemetery if we dont watch it too closely some time it will crawl into the cemetery or else crawl into the river and that will end all these wall street questions which are forever coming up

What are your ideas with regard to the Philippine Islands, Japan, China, Manchuria, the Open Door, the League of Nations, Mussolini, and the Gold Standard?

archy
the doctor has got me off of them he said i would either have to give them up or else lay off of gin and i could take my choice

but i will say as a general proposition i am opposed to them and it is my belief that sooner or later you will see them all down in union square getting clubbed by the cops which will prove that they are not respectable and to hell with anything not respectable has always been my motto

if george washington had got clubbed by the cops that would have proved he was a bolshevist and a communist and we would have heard very little more about him

Announcer:
What do you think of having a dictator for this country?

archy
that always comes down to a question of who bosses the dictator and i have very little time to give to that myself as i am full of literary projects

Announcer:
Do you believe the repeal of the anti-liquor laws has been an improvement?

archy
it may not have improved the country but it has improved the liquor

Announcer:
What did you think of the Russian five-year plan?

archy
i think it was a good thing and should be extended
five years more every five years indefinitely until it either
works or doesnt work which is all you want to know
about any plan
but i will say that in a general way i am very hopeful
not only about the future but about the past in looking
over the past i find a lot of swell things have happened
in the history of the world and today i find it far easier
to be optimistic about the past than about the future

Announcer:
Are you in favor of Fascism for this country?

archy
well i wouldnt say in favor of it exactly but i guess
at that it is a good deal handier than the old type of ice
box where the iceman has to drag the ice through the
kitchen and leaves little pools of water everywhere and
you forget to empty the pan and it spills over and runs
down through the ceiling of the room underneath

resurgam

look a here boss this thing
has gotta stop i
appeal to you for protection that
roughneck guy down cellar who
sent up the desiccated remnant of
a common chocolate colored water bug
and put it down by our typewriter
labeled exit archy is a person wholly
devoid of any real human
sensibility it
wasnt even decently preserved frag
mentary if you get what i mean when
my time to exit comes again i am
not going out that way in the cellar of
a printing shop i think i shall be a
humming bird next time or maybe i
shall take on something practical like
being a pawnbroker that depends a good
deal on how i am treated in this place
anyhow i am tired of this kind of
practical joke the reports of my exit
as uncle mark twain said are greatly
exaggerated

                                    archy

the ant bear

the ant bear may be toothless
but scorn not his capacity
his appetite is ruthless
his chief vice is edacity
he boasts without apology
his fad is entomology

                              archy

two comrades

i was walking in the park
the other day when i heard
a couple of fellows on a bench
exchanging ideas
the government says number one
ought to have these parks
air cooled in summer
yes and heat them in winter
says number two
how much longer says number one
are we going to stand for this
tyranny and oppression
no wonder communism is growing
they paid some friends of mine
not to raise pigs or potatoes
said number two
now i am off relief
and theyve got to pay me
not to raise hell
that sounds good said the other one
why couldnt we organize a racket
along those lines
poney up the jack or we will
become communists
suppose we give it a good patriotic
name like the defenders of
the constitution or something
i see by the papers that they are
going to spend millions for more
new roads
who the hell wants more auto roads
said his friend
there are roads enough now
what the poor man needs is more automobiles
to ride on them

and the government ought to give them to us
and the gasoline too
i refuse to help build roads
unless the government gives me a car
to use on them
they ought to give us chauffeurs too
said the other bum
they gotta give me a car
and a chauffeur or else
i will turn communist
if we could get paid by moscow
for turning communist
and get paid from washington
for not turning communist
it would just exactly suit me
we might weather it through
until good times come again
to hell with good times
said the other one
somebody is always shoving a job at you
in good times
what i used to suffer in good times
would draw tears from a stone
i never did so well in my life
as i have done during the recovery period
if us guys all stick together
we may be able to prevent
the return of good times
i doubt it said his friend
the damned capitalists
will sooner or later
be grinding us down under the
iron heel of prosperity again
boss i am glad i am
only an insect
and dont have to give myself headaches
trying to understand about
finance and economics and prosperity
and relief

                                    archy

*new deals and old deals and square deals
and ideals*

as the spiders wrote it

dear boss i met a spider
the other day in a museum
who gave me a good deal to think
about concerning governmental problems
this spider came of a long line of spiders
who had for thousands of years
inhabited the egyptian pyramids
and the american branch of the family
came over in a sarcophagus

along with the mummy
of one of the pharaohs

the ancient world saw all sorts
of governmental experiments
he said including monarchies
republics communes despotisms
democracies and everything else
but in the end the spiders got them all
thousands and thousands of years of
reforms and recoveries and depressions
and new deals and old deals
and square deals and crooked deals
and ideals and idealists
are wound around with spider webs
all the history of human kind
is written in the clots and filaments
and quaint patterns and ideographs
of spiders
it has been my observation
and experience and that of my family
that nothing human works out well
if you could read the writing
in the spider webs
you could understand the history of
human civilizations and understand
that man always fails because he
is not honest enough to succeed
there are not enough men
continuously on the square with
themselves and with other men
the system of government does not matter
so much the thing that matters
is what men do with any kind of system
they happen to have
many a time a strand of cobweb
has seemed to choke a burly empire to death
but the fact is that it was strangling anyhow
it was hanging itself in its own
crookedness and incompetence

there is no hope for human beings
unless they learn to organize their
social order as efficiently as spiders do
to say nothing of ants and bees
and coral insects

archy

a scarab

A cockroach seventy-four years old has been found
in a safe in Atchison—that is, Atchison claims that it is
seventy-four years old. We referred this matter to Archy
and he informed us:

i doubt if that
is really a cockroach
it sounds to me
more like an
egyptian scarab
cockroaches do not live
that long as a rule
i am the oldest
cockroach i know
and i am only sixty-three come
next michaelmas that is
in my present
incarnation

sell the glasses and make an additional profit

archy hunts a job

well boss i went up
to the circus
the other day
and tried to hire
out what do you
want they asked me a
job as an animal
or a job as an artist
an artist said i
what can you do they

said i can
walk the wire i said
either tight or slack
and i can swing
head downward from the
flying trapeze we do not
doubt it they said
but who could see
you at a distance
every one said i if you
gave them telescopes
and opera glasses it
is too expensive said they
to furnish opera
glasses to every one
just to see a cockroach
perform not at all
i said you sell the
glasses and make an
additional profit
you go out and hire
yourself out to a
trained flea outfit
said they we cannot use
you i consider it
an insult i replied to
be classed with
fleas you should consider
it a compliment said they
another word from you
i said and i
will die in a barrel
of your lemonade and
queer your show
and with this threat
the interview closed
                    archy

archy craves amusement

well boss
i am getting the
sandwich now but man
cannot live by buns alone
as the old soak will
learn some day what i want
is amusement i want
to go to the theater at least
once a week from now on
theaters are made
so that those who want to forget
will remember
and those who want to remember
will forget
but i think we need them
as much for fun as
for uplift

                              archy

fate is unfair

in many places here and
there
i think that fate
is quite unfair
yon centipede upon
the floor
can boast of
tootsies by the score
consider my
distressing fix
my feet are limited
to six

[316]

did i a hundred
feet possess
would all that glorious
footfulness
enable me
to stagger less
when i am
overcome by heat
or if i had
a hundred feet
would i
careering oer the floor
stagger
proportionately more
well i suppose
the mind serene
will not tell
destiny its mean
the truly
philosophic mind
will use
such feet as it can find
and follow calmly
fast or slow
the feet it has
where eer they go
                    archy

at the zoo

speaking of the aquarium i
was up at the zoo the
other day and when i saw all
the humans staring at
the animals i grew thankful that
i am an insect and
not an animal it must be
very embarrassing to
be looked at all the time by an
assorted lot of human beings and
commented upon as if
one were a freak the animals find the
humans just as strange and silly looking
as the humans find the
animals but they
cannot say so and the fact that
they cannot say so
makes them quite angry the leopard
told me that was one thing that
made the wild cat wild as for
himself he says there is
one gink that comes every day and looks
and looks and looks at him i
think said the leopard he
is waiting to see if i ever really do
change my spots

archy

no true friend

listen to me that
fellow who was in to see
you the other day bulling you
about your stuff
is no true friend you got
so proud of yourself on
account of what he
said you gave him a copy
of your book and
autographed it for him i thought
he was a shine so
i hopped into the
cuff of his trousers and
went out with him
he sold that book for
ten cents at a second
hand place and
treated himself to a
drink on the river front
he cursed because if
you had not written your name
in the book he might
have got fifteen cents for
it he said you are an
easy mark

                              archy

confessions of a glutton

after i ate my dinner then i ate
part of a shoe
i found some archies by a bathroom pipe
and ate them too
i ate some glue
i ate a bone that had got nice and ripe
six weeks buried in the ground
i ate a little mousie that i found
i ate some sawdust from the cellar floor
it tasted sweet
i ate some outcast meat
and some roach paste by the pantry door
and then the missis had some folks to tea
nice folks who petted me
and so i ate
cakes from a plate
i ate some polish that they use
for boots and shoes
and then i went back to the missis swell tea party
i guess i must have eat too hearty
of something maybe cake
for then came the earthquake
you should have seen the missis face
and when the boss came in she said
no wonder that dog hangs his head
he knows hes in disgrace
i am a well intentioned little pup
but sometimes things come up
to get a little dog in bad
and now i feel so very very sad
but the boss said never mind old scout
time wears disgraces out

                                        pete the pup

literary jealousy

dear boss i dont see
why you keep that ugly
boston bull terrier pete
hanging around
eating his head off
in these hard times
he is nothing but a parasite
and he has no morals
he has tried several times
to murder me

archy

When this ill-natured remark was read to Pete the Pup
he ambled over to the typewriter, got up on his hind legs
and pawed out the following reply:

i coNSIder It beneath
my Dignity to reply
to The sLanders of a Jealous
iNsect who does not
have a pUnctuaTION mark
in a baRRel of him
he is MereLY an archy
i am against anarchy
I AM A CAPITALIST
i wish to remind you however
that ONE STORY WHICH
YOU SOLD ABOUT ME BROUGHT
IN ENOUGH MONEY TO FEED ME
FOR FIVE YEARS AND I DENY
THAT I AM A PARASITE
moreover the time is
coming when you have to choose
between ME AND mehitabel
that lousy cat and when i say

LOusy i do not Mean the word
in iTS sLang SENSE
I mean Lousy in the sense of
a CAT wHo has LICE

                              pete the pup

pete at the seashore

i ran along the yellow sand
and made the sea gulls fly
i chased them down the waters edge
i chased them up the sky

i ran so hard i ran so fast
i left the spray behind
i chased the flying flecks of foam
and i outran the wind

an airplane sailing overhead
climbed when it heard me bark
i yelped and leapt right at the sun
until the sky grew dark

some little children on the beach
threw sticks and ran with me
o master let us go again
and play beside the sea

                              pete the pup

pete s theology

god made seas to play beside
and rugs to cover dogs
god made cars for holidays
and beetles under logs

god made kitchens so thered be
dinners to eat and scraps
god made beds so pups could crawl
under them for naps

god made license numbers so theyd find
lost pups and bring them home
god made garbage buckets too
to pry in when you roam

god made tennis shoes to chew
and here and there a hat
but i cant see why god should make
mehitabel the cat

                              pete the pup

and the cops watching all the time

pete petitions

when we are in the city we must walk
on streets all made of stone
with me upon a leash
and even in the park
i must not frisk or lark
and never run alone
without a muzzle on my jaws
and cops are watching all the time
lest i dig with my claws
and break some of their laws
and if i leap and bark

they act like i was bad
master i want some little towns
like we saw from the car
with meadows all about
where children romp and shout
brooks winding in and out
and nice bugs under stones
gardens to bury bones
and room to rip and race
and birds and cats to chase
trash cans to be tipped over
and grass to lie in and deep clover
and fence posts everywhere
no muzzles and no leashes there
and lots and lots of trees
o master buy a little town
where we can settle down
today o master please
buy me a little town
and a new rubber ball
and an ocean and thats all
right now o master please

pete the pup

pete s holiday

we found a hill all green with grass
and cool with clover bloom
where bees go booming as they pass
boom zoom boom

my master took me in the car
and high upon the hill
we lay and stared up at the clouds
until the day grew chill

and moths came floating from the sky
and shadows stroked the ground

and we lay still and stared and stared
and what do you think we found

we found a star between the clouds
upon the edge of night
but when i jumped and barked at it
it hid itself in fright

then we drove back to town again
with my head on his lap
it tires a dog to scare a star
and then he needs a nap

my master is the same as god
when he thumps with his hand
people bring us hamburg steaks
at any eating stand

o master let us go right now
and find another star
and eat another hamburg steak
at a refreshment bar

pete the pup

a radical flea

dear boss i wish you would speak
to that lazy good for nothing
boston bull terrier of yours
whom you call pete
pete has got the idea lately
that he is a great hunter
i saw him stage a dramatic battle
with a grass hopper yesterday
and he nearly won it too
and this morning he made an entirely
unprovoked attack on me
it was only by retreating into

the mechanism of your typewriter
that i saved my life
some day i will set mehitabel on him
she can lick any bull terrier who ever lived
she will make ribbons out of that pete
and they wont be dog show ribbons either
as for his pretensions to being a thoroughbred
i take no stock in them
i asked a flea of his about it
recently and the flea said
i doubt peters claim to aristocracy
very much he does not look like
an aristocrat to me
and more than that he does not taste like one
i have bit some pretty swell dogs
in my time and i ought to know
if pete is an aristocrat
then i am a bengal tiger
but in hard times like these
a flea has got to put up with
any kind of dog he can get hold of
back in 1928 when things were booming
i wouldnt look at anything
but a dachshund with a pedigree
as long as himself
if the government doesnt start
to putting out a better brand of dogs
at federal expense
a lot of us fleas are going
to turn communist in a big way
if there was any justice in this country
they would give us russian wolf hounds
i find a lot of discontent among
insects in these days

                                    archy

archy and the labor troubles

all right boss
i knuckle under
if you will not
pay me anything
for what i write
then you will not
i will return to the job
just to keep james the spider
out of it but all the
same it is cruel of you
to play upon the
jealousies
and susceptibilities
of artists in that fashion
i do not know how
you expect me to be
merry and bright
with this dull ache
of disillusionment at my
heart and the sharp
pang of hunger
in my stomach
some day i will plunge
into a mince pie
and mingle with its elements
and you will never see
me more and then
maybe you will begin
to appreciate
the poor little cockroach
who slaved that you might
live in comfort
maybe in spite of myself
i will haunt you then
if i were you i would hate

to be haunted by the ghost
of a cockroach
think of it boss
everywhere you looked
to see a spectral cockroach
that none but you knew was
there to pick him from
your shirt front when
others were blind to him
to feel him crawling
on your collar in public
places to be compelled
to brush him from your plate
when you sat down to dine
to pluck him always from the glass
before you dared to drink
to extend your hand
to grab that of some fair
lady and then hesitate and
pick him from her wrist
people would begin to think
you were a little
queer boss and if you
attempted to explain
they would think you still
queerer what in the world
is the matter with you
they would say
oh nothing nothing at all
you would answer
plucking at the air
it will soon pass i merely
thought i saw a cockroach
on your nose madam
suspicions of your sanity
would grow and grow
do you not like that
pudding your hostess would ask
and you would murmur
being taken off your guard

it is very good pudding
indeed i was just
trying not to eat
the cockroach
boss i do not make
any threats at all
i just simply state what
may very well happen to
you through remorse if you
drive me to suicide
i will try not to
haunt you boss because
i am loving and forgiving
in my spirit but who
knows that i will not be
compelled to haunt you
in spite of myself
a hard heart will not get
you anything boss
remember the plagues
of egypt perhaps to
your remorseful mind i
will be multiplied
by millions i am giving
you a last chance to
repent you should be glad
that i am only a cockroach
and not a tarantula
yours prophetically

                                    archy

an ultimatum

boss this is my
ultimatum unless you have
made arrangements
for more regular meals for
me by monday
september 18 i will
quit you cold and go out and
live in a
swiss cheese i have nothing
to arbitrate

                archy

no snap

say boss its a good
thing for you
that you dont pay me any wages for
the stuff i write
for you if you did
i would have to have them raised all
these strikes are getting
me feverish and excited one of
my long pieces in your column
often costs me twelve or
fifteen hours of steady
labor and i am drowsy
all the next day butting these
keys with my head is no snap boss
anything i got for it would
be underpaying me i wish you would
buy a pear and leave it under the
metal typewriter case where the rats
cant get to it

                archy

he gets in bad

say boss i had
a great idea last night i thought
if i could operate a
typewriter why not a
linotype machine i went down into
the composing room
and started to hop from key to key
and a guy said to me wheres
your union card
get out of here or you will get
into the paper
in a way you dont like you will
get a nice hot bath
in that little pot of type metal do
you get me you may con the editorial
staff but no unpunctuated
gink can sling his joshbillingsgate
around here see
raus or i will spread you on
the minutes and not charge
any overtime for it
either so i came away

archy

and i would like a little automobile

economic

boss i should like
to discuss one or two
business matters with you
quite seriously
in the first place i need
some sort of head gear such as
football players wear
i have to butt each
key of the typewriter
with my head
and i am developing

callouses on my brain
these callouses on my
brain are making me cruel
and careless in my thoughts
i am becoming brutal
almost human
in my writings
and then i would like
a little automobile
i have to go from place
to place so much
picking up news for you
a clock work one would do
with a chauffeur to keep it
wound up for me
and a lightning bug to
sit in front and be
the headlight on dark nights
i hate to mention food boss
it seems so sordid
and plebeian but i no longer
find any left over crusts
of sandwiches in your
waste paper basket i am
forced to haunt the
restaurants and hotels for food
and this is at the
imminent risk of my life
unless i get these things
i will quit you on
november first is not the
laborer worthy of his hire
yours for economic justice
and a living wage

archy

archy revolts

We have received the following communication from Archy:

                    i refuse to endorse
                    the idea of
                    an archy week
                    which you have advertised
                    in your column
                    i will not march
                    down fifth avenue
                    at the head of any
                    procession
                    i will not take part
                    in any silly celebration
                    i am a serious artist
                    i do not exploit
                    myself and i shall not
                    permit myself to be exploited
                    i do the best work
                    i am capable of
                    and i do not care
                    for any contact with the
                    public except upon
                    the printed page
                    i shall not go on
                    lecture tours
                    or attend dinners
                    or soul and uplift fights
                    i do not care to
                    have persons whose opinions
                    i do not respect
                    telling me that they admire
                    my work and have so yearned
                    to meet me
                    i refuse to act as the bait

at affairs
where social and literary
climbers hope to
attract celebrities
by advertising that
i am one of the guests of honor
i shall neither
write nor speak
nor allow my name to be used
for the benefit
of causes that i do not care
a damn about
i shall not answer letters
from persons who write to me
for no other object
than to have me answer
their letters
my time when i am not working
is my own
my work is all that
the public is entitled to know
about me
it is all the public pays for
i shall not
allow my name to be used
by committees
that are framing
up organizations of one kind
or another
because i do not care
whether there is
another organization
of any sort ever comes
into existence in the world
i shall not spend money
having photographs taken
to give away to people
who are too stingy
to buy them from
photographers but hope

to graft them off of me
you can take
your archy week
and go and jump off the dock
with it tucked
under your arm
and i shall stand on shore
and watch you and it
sink for the third time
with a smile on my face
now that you know
where you get off
please go and get off there
i am a serious artist
i repeat
and will have nothing
to do with any
of the current form
of cheap publicity
                    archy

archy wants a change

well boss the time
has come when
you and i
will have to have
some kind of a
showdown
for years i have been
working for you
and doing a large
share of your work
without getting a cent
of pay for it
some of your best
ideas have been my ideas and you have
not given me
credit for them
you have not even
fed me boss
for two years now
formerly you used to
eat sandwiches in
your office and
i could get a crumb
now and then from
the waste basket
but since you have been
trying to reduce
your weight
for the tenth time
in three years you
no longer eat
in the office i have
been your faithful
slave and you have made a thousand
promises to me and

kept none of them
when i went on strike
for my rights
you did not take it
seriously
now i have determined
to quit you unless
you do something for
me i want to go
to paris i have
always wanted to go
to paris and i
demand that you
take me and take
me soon otherwise i will
leave you flat
a word to the
wise is sufficient

                              archy

Needless to say, we shall ignore this preposterous demand on the part of Archy. If he wants to quit us, it will
be good riddance of bad rubbish.

archy on strike

We have received a communication from Archy, who went on strike forty-eight hours ago, desiring us to state that he is not backed by any association of contributors but that he is striking on his own initiative. We think it is only fair to the poor misguided cockroach to give his statement to the public. We do not print it as a contribution from him, because, until he has formally withdrawn the outrageous demands which he made upon us the other day, no article signed by him shall appear ever again. To print signed articles by him would be, in effect, to recognize his organization; and this we shall never do.

We present an article by a new cockroach named Henry. Henry has not had as much practice at the typewriter keyboard as Archy, and he manages to hit a capital letter now and then, without always being able to hit the right capital; but we can assure our readers that he is learning rapidly. Henry is at least trying to punctuate; Archy always made the contention that no cockroach could ever learn to punctuate and refused to try. Archy's failure to punctuate influenced a great many persons against him. Henry may be a little more difficult than Archy was, for a few days, but he is ambitious and in the end he will be better than Archy.

We present Henry:

a communication from henry

> well, be asTH,is is? seerious
> allthis labor dis CONtent
> I wonders wHere IT wiLL enD
> i sh ould not
> CarE toprophesy?
> but the greaTest dePrivation i

[340]

feel, is in t he Loss OF thE
suBway sUn i usEd 2 GET a LL
   my NEWS froM the Subway suN but,
   siNce the subWAY has stop ped.
   ruNNINg iaM at a LosS!
   How wiLl We kNow the strike has
   ended. if weDo noT reAd IT in
   thesubwaY Sun
      And How wilL we Read thesubwAY
      suN unleSS The sTrike
   ends. i WISH u would watcH
      mehitaBEL the CAT? she IS
   jEalous anD soRe because i
   haVE taken arcHy?s j oB
      And calLS me a scaB and
   Last niGht tried to
   eat me i deMAND poLice proTectioN?
                        heNry!

All statements made by Mehitabel the Cat, with regard to the strike of Archy, are to be viewed with suspi-
cion. Her statement that she is herself on strike is false on
the face of it, as Mehitabel has never been employed by
this column, although she has occasionally been interviewed for it.

It seems not improper to state that Archy, himself, is
picketing the office, and last evening when Henry left
work Archy stopped him and made threats against him.
Henry is very well able to take care of himself, but we
have asked for a special police detail to protect him.

If Archy introduces the element of violence into the
strike, he will be severely dealt with!

how the public viewed the strike

SIR: Now that Archy is gone, you may be able to get out a readable column again.—R.P.

SIR: Unless you can fix it up with Archy, count me off the subscription list. I hate to hurt anybody's feelings, but I would rather see you take a long vacation yourself than to lose Archy.—WALT.

SIR: Unless you accede to Archy's just demands all your readers will go on a sympathetic strike. It matters not about the other contributors. Let C. B. Gilbert, Benjamin DeCasseres, and Clinton Scollard go. Or go yourself. But we gotter have Archy.—ELIZABETH.

SIR: There are three ways that the deplorable strike of Archy may end:
He may win.
You may win.
Or the pair of you may compromise.
I must say that I was horrified at the brutal capitalistic attitude taken up by you towards one of the brightest ornaments of modern American literature.—F.J.C.

poem from henry

liFe is Not aLL jazz and Joy)
     sMiles and suNNy weaTher!
EVERy golD has it'S aLloy!
toHOld tHe Stuff together!

!if LUCk is good! why maN aliVE!
     weLcoMe iT! And ch eer iT!
buT if THE drinK'S two seven five
     Try to griN! AND beer iT!
          heNry!

Henry strikes us as being, on the whole, more cheerful than Archy.

As Henry left work last evening, he was attacked by a strange cockroach, no doubt a thug in the employ of Archy, who has been hanging about the building ever since Henry went on the job. The strange cockroach was easily disposed of, and Archy did not show himself in person.

We repeat what we said yesterday: If Archy is foolish enough to introduce violence into this strike, he will get his fill of it.

It has been reported to us that Archy has been drinking wood alcohol and is working himself into a rage against Henry. Candidly, we expect the worst. But the column is not to be intimidated.

progress of the strike

There is no offering from Henry today. Henry has disappeared. Frankly, we fear that Henry has been foully dealt with by a gang of rowdy cockroaches in the employ of Archy.

The column made an attempt at an early hour this morning to put another cockroach named Ernatz to work. Ernatz arrived at the office and succeeded in getting as far as the typewriter, but there he collapsed. An examination showed that Ernatz had been badly beaten up by the Archy faction in getting through the picket lines.

These picket lines have been extended by Archy and his gang until they now reach from the Press Club at Spruce and William up Spruce Street to Nassau, and down Nassau to what used to be the Umbrella Bar at the corner of Nassau and Beekman. We were informed today by an excited friend that he had seen thousands and thousands and thousands of cockroaches, led by Archy, hiding by the curbstones picketing this district, and that it seemed to him that they were maddened by benzine or something. They had chased him, he said, and he was so extraordinarily vivid and convincing in his recital and in his fright that we fancied, as he talked, that we could actually smell the benzine or something.

The column's cockroach service has been interrupted for one day; but it will be resumed. We ask the public to be patient. As far as taking Archy back is concerned, that is now an impossibility; we are done with that ingrate forever.

a threat

We found on our desk this morning the following threat from the Archy faction, which we publish to show the public the length to which this creature is willing to go:

> unless you yield to
> archys demands the strike
> will spread the water bugs
> are going out in
> sympathy with archy and the
> vers libre poets union
> are preparing a sympathetic
> strike the public will know whom
> to blame they will blame you
> it is your capitalistic
> attitude that is
> prolonging the trouble take
> warning by what
> happened to henry and ernatz

So far the Mayor, the District Attorney, and the Governor have done nothing—less than nothing. We demand protection for our contributors, or we shall have a word or two to say about these officials. Several of our contributors have been threatened—C. B. Gilbert, Benjamin DeCasseres, Edward S. Van Zile, H. W., Edward Hope, and the Editor of the column have all received threatening letters from the Archy faction.

Whither is this country drifting?

The column hesitates to adopt the expedient of employing strikebreakers and guards for the purpose of getting contributors through the Archy lines; but if it becomes necessary, it shall be done. A dozen tarantulas have been offered to us by a steamship company which maintains a line of boats between this port and South and Central America, and unless the cockroaches cease to interfere with our employees, or the proper authorities wake up and give us protection, we shall be obliged to accept this offer.

the public and the strike

SIR: Restore the Archytect who made the column famous. Our Monarchy forever!!!—J.U.N.

SIR: I was amused at the suggestion of F.J.C. that Archy might win. The poor cockroach hasn't even the chances of the proverbial snowball or the tallow cat hotly pursued by the asbestos pup. His chances are about those of law clerks on strike. My sympathies are with Archy as they surely are with law clerks, but roaches and law schools are equally prolific.—J.C.

SIR: Your column has so deteriorated that I shall never buy another paper until this Archy business is settled in Archy's favor.—STEADY READER.

> Don't let Archy pine and die,
>   We miss his gracious art,
> Don't grudge him half an apple pie;
>   Recall him; have a heart!
>
> Let me subscribe a dozen pies
>   And keep the column bright—
> Call Archy back and compromise
>   Or kiss yourself good-night!
>   H.D.

SIR: This is to give you formal notice that unless Archy is reinstated within forty-eight hours the entire reportorial staff of the newspaper will walk out. It seems almost incomprehensible that anyone should throw over a cultured cockroach like Archy, one who shows the breeding and refinement of the butler's pantry, for a low thing like Henry, who has probably spent most of his life roaming over musty pies and concrete doughnuts in Park Row basement restaurants.—E.B.

SIR: Siding entirely with Archy in his fight for living wages, if you will kindly give me his address in your daily column I will get in touch with him and induce him to accept a good position with a newspaper published by a large exporting firm. Do you think he would be averse to soliciting advertisements from any kind of people who may be willing to come across with the dough?

M. DE LA PENA.

SIR: The truth about Archy's strike: I myself have been threatened by a strike of my characters—Craig Kennedy, Walter Jameson, and all. Archy is the walking delegate in the strike of contribs.

I have a proposal for us authors. I propose that we apply to the American Federation of Labor for a charter ourselves—the Central Federated Union of Authors, Local No. 1. We will not insist on the closed shop at once, but that will come ultimately. The final goal must be the super-closed shop—every reader of a book or magazine, every spectator at a picture show or theater must belong to the union. Toward this glorious ideal Archy has taken the first step. I hope he pickets your scab column and puts it on the "unfair" list. Better come on in—the water's fine.

ARTHUR B. REEVE.

SIR: As a strike breaker Henry was a mighty poor pick, unless he was all the detective agency had to furnish. If you were not such an impetuous boss you might have discovered this before putting your foot down on Archy's moderate demands. It would be just as well before you go further to let a pile driver drop on all there is of the pretentious Henry. A friend of Archy's tells me that Archy's back is much stiffened since he has seen the quality of his substitute's work. And this friend doesn't think that either the Governor, the Mayor, the District Attorney, the Corporation Counsel, the Public Service Commissioner, the Police Commissioner, the Inspector of Garbage, or all combined can induce Archy to arbitrate. Indeed it is believed that Archy is preparing something really drastic, in case you should be willing to capitulate before the end of the week. I am sure you can save your face now better than you will be able to later on.

You gotta give in. Another time don't be so quick to monkey with the bug-saw.

A Friend of Both.

Sir: Let me be the "Obvious Adams" in the Archy strike. I buy the paper every night at two cents. It is obvious that my total expenditure for the week is twelve cents. It is further obvious that a piece of pie of the dimensions demanded by Archy costs but ten cents. Therefore it is obvious that you can pay his demands and still work at a profit.

Until the strike is decided in Archy's favor I shall continue to read your paper over the shoulder of my fellow passenger, or, I will subscribe to the *Subway Sun.*

This is final!

Iggie.

Sir: I congratulate you on having got rid of Archy. Now maybe we can have some more Fothergil Finch. And what has become of Hermione, the Beautiful communist? Seriously, I have always felt that Archy was beneath the dignity of the column.

W. F. Marner.

archy gets a 50 per cent increase

Archy agreed this morning to return to work, for at least a week, pending a final adjustment of the difficulties between him and the column.

Archy's demands were for a piece of apple pie once a week and for larger type for his contributions.

These demands will be considered in the final adjustment.

In the meantime, and pending the final adjustment, Archy returns on the basis of a 50 per cent increase in salary.

It is our contention that a 50 per cent increase is a very liberal increase, indeed, and that this temporary settlement should be a permanent settlement.

We admit that the public has been with Archy during the recent troubles. And it was only the pressure of public opinion that influenced us to take him back at all.

But, having decided that we must yield, we determined to come across handsomely.

THE 50 PER CENT INCREASE IN SALARY WAS OUR OWN SUGGESTION.

AND, ON OUR OWN INITIATIVE, WE HAVE MADE THIS INCREASE RETROACTIVE.

That is to say, not only does Archy get the 50 per cent increase during the week before the final adjustment, but we have volunteered to give it to him during the period covered by the strike, and for a term of two weeks prior to the strike.

SIR: Since Archy first became prominent as a literary bug, I have followed him through all his travels and adventures with fascinated interest. To me his vicissitudes have been a continuous source of enjoyment. And now that you have forced this poor downtrodden creature to abandon you to your own puny talents, may you live to regret it. Tomorrow when I open my paper, if **Archy** does not appear in the newspaper, I shall clip your column and burn it publicly with due and proper ceremony. —Gus.

We print, below, Archy's own comment upon the temporary settlement:

comment from archy

well boss you see
where you stand now i hope the
public cannot get along
without me
i have won a moral victory
for you have agreed in
principle that i
should have a raise in
salary i will have to
think over it a
long time however before i
will consent to a 50 per cent
raise as a permanent settlement
and will have to take
advice it seems like a very
generous proposition on the
face of it but at the same time
i dont think it is
altogether right the figures look
good but i am puzzled you
see i was not getting any salary at
all when i quit work and if
i got a raise of
50 per cent above that the
question is what do i get
i would much rather have a
little something to eat every
week than all these figures but

                    at the same time i
                    must admit that a 50 per cent
                    raise looks good
                    on paper especially as you are
                    willing to make it
                    retroactive maybe the
                    retroactive part means that i
                    will get a little something
                    to eat at any rate it is easy
                    to see that i have won a most
                    important victory i would be willing
                    to make a permanent
                    settlement on the basis of
                    a 25 per cent increase and a half
                    a piece of pie i never was any good on
                    figures and maybe i am
                    getting a lot as it is but i
                    would rather have less
                    of a victory and more to eat

                                        archy

   We print this communication in full in order to show
the public the difficulty we have with Archy. We have
yielded in principle, we admit that he has won a victory, and we have given him a 50 per cent raise. It
seems to me that we have done even more than could
have been expected, but he seems dissatisfied. And yet
he must know that he is in the wrong, for even while he
talks of a moral victory he reduces his former outrageous
demands for food by one half. He has been on the job
without any food at all, so far as we know, for four years,
and this sudden demand of his for something to eat does
not have the ring of sincerity to our ears. What did he
eat before he worked for the column? There is a strain
of sordid materialism in Archy, we are afraid.

                    well i note you
                    put me back into nonpareil
                    again monday after raising me
                    to brevier all right boss

                          [350]

all right grind down
the laboring man there will come
a day of reckoning i dont have
to do this you know as far
as the food is concerned that
you have been giving me i lived before
i ever got into your column must close now
as mehitabel the cat is
scratching her claws against
the desk in a meaning sort of way
yours hastily

                                        archy

a conversation with archy

insects and
the so called lower
animals have practically
no vices at all
as compared
with human beings

                        archy

Yes, yes, Archy; but does that prove the superiority of
insects and the so-called lower animals? Or does it seem
to point toward the necessity of vice in the evolutionary
scheme? And to say "the necessity of vice" is to say "the
necessity of morals"; for where there are no morals there
is no vice.

well well
you do not feel
very sure of your
position or you would
not condescend to argue
about it with an insect
there is another thing
which i would like

            to bring up
            while we are talking
            frankly to each other
            and that is
            the question of my raise
            i returned to work faithfully
            on the understanding
            that i was to be fed
            occasionally
            but you never leave
            anything on your desk any more
                                archy

We give you an opportunity to express yourself, and
for the true artist that should be enough. You are always
talking about your devotion to your art.

                i want to be paid more
                where would you be
                if i left you flat
                the only ideas
                you ever had
                you got from me
                and after this i want
                to appear in ten point
                type
                                archy

After this you appear in minion type, or you don't
appear at all.

                just listen to this then
                this is my ultimatum
                unless this piece
                i am now writing
                appears in ten point
                type i will never
                write another line
                for you
                                archy

Just for that it goes in minion. And we are not afraid of your quitting us, again. We know that expression is the great need of your soul, and that rather than not get the publicity you would take it even in agate.

>   i want to say just
>   one more word before
>   i get through with you
>   forever
>   and that is that you
>   are a damned ingrate
>   i made you what you are
>   and this is the treatment
>   you give me
>   archy

That outburst of rebellion reduces you to nonpareil.

>   all right
>   good by forever
>   archy

You see what trying to bully us gets you! Your fare-well is in agate. No cockroach can intimidate us! And if you ever come back into the column you come back in pearl type, and work your way up again. The suggestion of pay for contributions is repulsive and bolshevistic. Columns simply are not done that way.

>   well this goes into
>   brevier type instead of nonpareil
>   if you keep your promise thank
>   you for the raise in salary boss
>   but i find i have not
>   anything of great moment
>   to say how often that
>   happens when a man becomes
>   conspicuous he has used all
>   his best stuff winning fame in

[353]

small type or some other
inconspicuous way and in
poverty and obscurity has put his
soul into his work suddenly fame
and success come and he gets promoted
to big type on account of his
merits and lo and behold his
great thoughts desert him thank you
for the raise i hope the common fate
will not overtake me boss i will
strive to deserve the raise
hereafter

archy

Just for this, you go in agate, Archy.

see here boss i am no kicker nor
growler nor do i want more than is coming
to me but after raising me to brevier one
day you slammed me back into nonpareil
again what i want to know is this if you
think the stuff is rotten why do you
use it at all and if you think it is o k
why not give it a show here i am
trying to build up a public for
myself and you too and look at the
appreciation i get all right boss all right
but i warn you that you are queering your
own game i dont ask for brevier this time
but you might at least give me minion if
i make good in minion then raise me think
it over then think it over i am making no
threats of quitting but you think it over

archy

well boss i notice that
although you have taken me
back to work on my own terms
you are giving me no
work to do you always were jealous

[354]

of my popularity there
never has been a time since i made
my first appearance and
carried all before me that you
would not have gotten rid of
me if you had dared but
you have never dared
now you are giving me no work to do
in order to keep me
from my public you are
trying to ruin me why do
you not give me an
assignment now and
then

                              archy

If Archy cannot think up something to write about he
can stay out of the column permanently. We are tired
of giving Archy assignments that he can do easily and
then having him take the credit for originality. The im-
pression has gone abroad that not only does Archy think
up his own themes, but that he also tells us what to write.
The exact reverse of this is true. It is time that Archy,
and his infatuated followers also, should understand that
he is our subordinate, our creature. We admit that he has
a certain superficial knack; but all the heavier, more
solemn, respectable, and serious humor in the column is
our own. His statement that he would like to work is entirely hypocritical. Since he won the strike he has done
nothing but eat and sleep; he is gorged with food; between his triumph and his victuals he has become stupid.
We knew food would ruin him, and it was in the interests of his literary ability, such as it is, that we kept him
starved. Lord Tennyson noticed the same thing about
a throstle . . . or maybe it was a blackbird. Anyhow, Lord
Tennyson wrote a poem about it. . . . It was a bird that
gorged itself and lived easy and ceased to be a poet. We
have always thought it an indication of very high purpose and resolution that Lord Tennyson did not succumb
himself in a similar manner; but after he became laure-

ate he sang just as well as before. We believe that he was already laureate when he wrote "Come into the Garden, Maud." Max Beerbohm has a cartoon of Lord Tennyson reading his poems to Queen Victoria in which the laureate looks both well fed and lyrical. We wish that Daisy Ashford's Mr. Saltena had met a laureate at court and given us additional light upon this subject. But we still insist that in spite of Lord Tennyson's experience, the rule holds good in the majority of cases; feed a poet and ruin him. The only thing that can save Archy now is a course of voluntary fasting, and we doubt that he has the will power for it. Give a cockroach enough jam and he will tangle his feet.

archy gets restless again

dear boss after thinking
over the terms of our temporary
settlement i
am forced to admit i
got the short end of the
deal you are a true diplomat and
a modest one at that but i want
you to know that your admission
to your readers in conceding me
a moral victory does not
suffice to fill an empty
stomach and nobody can work
without food so i am forced to
submit as the two chief subjects for
consideration in the final settlement the
necessity not only for deciding the
amount of salary but also a generous
allowance of food and good
food at that because since i
agreed to return to work i
met an old friend who took me to

a place where a lot of
nice people of the community
councils are distributing relief
food and by simply hiding in the
parcels that go out there are
lots of chances to get into all
kinds of fine homes we took a chance
and sneaked into one box of canned
goods and were placed in a fine
automobile that took us
to a swell house on the drive where
they have a pastry cook of their own and
we had the pastry all to our
selves and feasted on delicacies of
all sorts so half a piece of pie is
no longer any treat for me and
i can get acquainted with
some very aristocratic
cockroaches besides just by
attending food sales and i
am cultivating a taste for fancy
eatables that neither pie nor
25 per cent increase will satisfy

                                        archy

It looks as if this Archy were getting ready to ask for
more, no matter what we give him.
   How human some cockroaches are!

                    say
                    maybe those guys
                    who are always
                    urging you
                    onward towards labor
                    and toil
                    and work and industry
                    just simply need
                    the money
                    your work produces
                                        archy

seldom do i meet a person who will hold
still long enough for me to get a meal

the cockroaches are not
the only insects
that are demanding more
consideration
i met a flea
last evening who
told me that he had come
into contact with
a great deal of unrest
lately and a mosquito remarked
to me only this
morning there is darned
little justice in this world the

way the human beings
run it seldom do i
meet a person who will hold
still long
enough for me to get a meal
                              archy

archy triumphs

thank you for the
advice to go and get
some of this
government food i do
not want to start all
over again
any controversy that has
been temporarily
settled but may i not
ask how
                              archy

well boss the time has
arrived for our permanent
settlement i propose
a plum plan
once a week i want a
pint jar of plum preserves
with bread and butter
and all the fixings that
go with them answer at once
i refuse to arbitrate
                              archy

We yield. We consider ourself lucky that Archy does
not demand full ownership and control of the column.
We yield while the yielding is still good.

boss i see by the
papers that there is

one income tax slacker who
owes 14 800 000 dollars lest
there be any possibility of
mistake i wish to state
publicly that i am not the
person the salary i receive for
my writings in the column
falls considerably below that
figure even in good
years yours for
vers libre as usual

archy

yes we have

i heard a good
story the other
day boss
i wonder if
you have heard it stop
me if you have wont you
it seems that
two cabbies in london
had had a bad day
it was raining
like anything and
neither one of them
had picked up a
fare in hours
have you heard it
they were driving along
side by side
bloodying their luck
when suddenly an old lady
came out of a house
and signaled to them
do you know it
they both stepped on the gas

neither of them had picked up a fare

and made
a mad dash for her
arriving at the same time
they drew
up before her
shes mine shouted one of
them at the top of his
lungs
im rotten at this
cockney dialect
like ell she
is shes mine hollered
the other

garn howled his rival
i seen the old bitch
first didnt i lady

archy

a wail from little archy

i can walk on six feet
or i can walk
on four feet
maybe if i tried hard enough
i could walk on two feet
but i cannot
walk on five feet
or on three feet
or any odd number of feet
it slews me around
so that i go catercornered
i mention this because
of my present
distressing condition
you have not fed
me lately let alone paying
me anything and
last night while eating
an apple core
in your waste paper basket
three of my feet
froze fast to it and are
useless at present writing
i wish you would
give me a set of galoshes
for my annual salary i
do not expect
real food from you any more
you always treat me
as if i were a constituent
and you were a politician

that my vote had just
elected to office
i dont know why i keep on
working for you
it is either a habit or a vice
                                    archy

doing well

as i was
crawling through
a shoe store the
other day i
heard two pairs of shoes
talking to each other
well says the
first pair
you neednt feel
so smart
you have been
marked down from
twenty dollars to sixteen
while i have been marked
down from twenty one
dollars to
eighteen dollars
well said the
second pair i
make no claims to
superiority but
i will say i think
we are both doing
damned well for
five dollar shoes

                                    archy

takes talent

there are two
kinds of human
beings in the world
so my observation
has told me
namely and to wit
as follows
firstly
those who
even though they
were to reveal
the secret of the universe
to you would fail
to impress you
with any sense
of the importance
of the news
and secondly
those who could
communicate to you
that they had
just purchased
ten cents worth
of paper napkins
and make you
thrill and vibrate
with the intelligence

                              archy

summer is icumen in

my scouts
from all over
the country tell
me that it is
getting along
towards the time
of year
when plump ladies
sit around
on the verandas
of summer hotels
and boarding houses
and swap
interesting yarns
about the times
they have been
under the knife
of the surgeon

archy

greetings old feather duster said i

archy climbs everest

may fifteenth nineteen
thirty five started climbing
mount everest early this morning
met the maharajah of nepal one hundred feet **up**
greetings old feather duster said i
that is not a feather duster he said
that is
stop i cried dont you tell me
that is your wife
that is my beard he said

i accept the apology i said
quick as a flash

may sixteen at one thousand feet
i met an avalanche coming down
as i was going up
we compromised and this morning
i am starting all over again
dancing on the avalanche
as it skidded towards sea level
were two strange figures
prancing on their hind legs
whom i identified as the dalai lama

mehitabel once was a hindu nun

and mehitabel the cat
they were singing in part as follows
oh the lama here
is a son of a gun
and mehitabel once
was a hindu nun
skip skip my himalaya honey
the rarefied air
of the mountain side
has completely withered
the lamas pride
hike hike my himalaya honey
if the bottom of the hills
were placed at the top
when we wanted to go up
wed merely have to drop
drill drill my himalaya honey

may seventeen oh lord
the maharajah of nepal
is following me with a squirt gun
full of insect poison
here comes another avalanche

                                              archy

archy on everest

may eighteenth fifteen
thousand feet up on mount
everest today i caught a ride
on an airplane going my way
everyone i meet is all hopped up
with the altitude
caught up with the maharajah of nepal
gaily hopping over the snow and ice
bare legged i said to him
hello spinach face are you starting
a nudist colony up here
and he replied
an avalanche
tore off my panche
and left me feeling funny
but we never rest
on everest
my himalaya honey
yes i says but who was that lady
i seen you walking with
a mile or so below
that wasnt no lady he says quick as a flash
that was the taj mahal
skipping along ahead of us were
the dalai lama and mehitabel the cat
mehitabel had written in the snow
send a message to my public
in america please archy give them
love and kittens from mehitabel
and the dalai lama
may nineteenth spent the day
riding up in airplanes
and coasting down on avalanches
if you dont know anything about asia
it would surprise you how much traffic

there is in the himalayas
may twentieth twenty thousand feet up
overtook a bum who says he is
nicholas romanoff formerly czar
of all the russias and when i say all
i mean all archy he said
the sun never set on my dominions
why not i asked him
because they were too cold
to hatch he replied ask me another
the reds missed me he said
and i have been in siberia ever since
i figure if i can get to the top
and stay there i will be safe
have you got a can opener
what for i enquired
i have some canned heat he said
but i cant get into it
i have practically lived on canned heat
ever since i escaped from russia
may twenty first got carried down
four thousand feet by a snow slide
when i came to myself
i was on a ledge of rock
and sitting in a row with their feet
hanging over nothing were mehitabel the cat
the dalai lama and the taj mahal
nicholas romanoff and the maharajah of nepal
all drinking canned heat and singing
in part as follows
we have tried all sorts
of winter sports
and spent a mint of money
we have skied the alps
and cracked our scalps
and burrowed like a bunny
but everest is sure the best
my himalaya honey
listen now said the former czar
and i will tell you the story of my life

it was going off of gold that ruined me
you mean the gold standard asked the lama
no said the maharajah
he means the gold cure
nevertheless said nicholas romanoff
i will tell you now the
story of my life
with slides asked the taj mahal
cant you try and forget it
mister romanoff asked the maharajah
no said the former czar
sniffing the canned heat
not while i have this rosemary
it is for remembrance
and he hit his insides
a terrific wallop with the horrid stuff
yes and rue is for you
said the taj mahal
kicking him five thousand feet downhill
and larkspur is for cooties
the dalai lama shouted
after him as he whirled into space
i discovered a virgin gold mine
the next morning how do you know
it is virgin asked mehitabel
yes said the taj mahal explain
tush tush said the dalai lama
give it the benefit of the doubt
well it seems reasonable said i
there is a snow slide
over it every twenty minutes

                                        archy

and the result was hamlet

archy on the theater

Archy the Cockroach crawled into my office late the other night, scurried to my typewriter, and butted out the following ungenerous remark:

> the theater is lousy
> these days lousier than
> it has been in three hundred years

"And what do you know about it?" I asked him.

> i know everything about it
> my ancestors have lived in theaters

for centuries
i am the repository of thousands
of generations of theatrical tradition
one of my ancestors was living
contentedly in a pile of old scripts
when a manager jerked one out
from underneath him one day
and handed it to a guy named shakespeare
and said bill get this old
junk into shape so we can
start rehearsals on it next tuesday
stick in a couple of murders
and some of your low browed comedy
and your smutty wisecracks
and philosophical hokum
and i dont need to tell you what to do
and the result was a play called hamlet
and another of my ancestors
was living in kit marlowes
fine elizabethan ruff
getting fat on starch
when marlowe was writing doctor faustus
my family has always lived around
theaters and theatrical hangouts
and one of my grandfathers grandfathers
used to live in edwin booths room
at the players club under the rug
and i repeat again that the theater
these days is lousy

"What's the matter with it?" I asked him. And the insignificant insect replied, at length, as follows:

no glamour no illusion
that has all been thrown out of doors
and the movies have picked it up
and are doing the best they can with it
in their bungling way
the movies are struggling in a dumb headed

thumb handed way to give the public
some escape from the realities of life
and a glimpse into the fourth dimension
but the legitimate stage
goes right on presenting
stereotyped patterns of what is called
realism by which it means
the surface of the lives
of insignificant people
the reason the movies are doing business
and the theater is not
is not altogether one of price
or the financial condition of the country
the movies are young and crude
and are not afraid of gusto and the heroic
whether they sentimentalize
some lousy gunman and his doings
or put across an incredible western
or splurge with hokum melodrama
or embark on an adventure
of pure phantasy like walt disneys stuff
they are instinctively trying
to hand the public some kind of stuff
that wins the audience away from
the sordid surface of existence
they may do it badly
they may do it obviously
they may do it crudely
but they do have the hunch
that what the millions want is to be shown
that there is something possible
to the human race
besides the dull repetition
of the triviality which is the routine
of common existence

"You can certainly use some highbrow expressions,
when you set yourself to it, Archy," I said to the incredible cockroach. But the conceited insect kept right on butting his opinions out on the keyboard.

```
                the legitimate stage
                is afraid of ranting
                the legitimate stage is afraid
                of any breadth of gesture
                the legitimate stage is afraid
                of being kidded if it puts across
                a genuine fervor of emotion
                it is all tightened up and narrowed down
                by its various fears
                but the movies from the start
                have had to please the millions
                in order to exist in a business way
                and they have had to keep in touch
                with the mind of the mob
                and the mob always wants a hero in a story
                with whom it can identify itself
                in some attempt to break through
                into a better condition of existence
                the great fault of the movies
                has also been their great virtue
                that is their necessity to cater to millions
                it has compelled them to keep in touch
                with the modern equivalent of folk lore
                every now and then they have blundered
                into doing something with a touch
                of the universal in it just
                because they follow ignorantly
                this instinctive hunch of theirs
```

Archy ceased to write, and held his head with four of
his feet. I thought he was grieving for the condition of
the theater, and asked him if this was the case.

```
                no he said
                the theater has deserted me
                and i am willing to let it go
                it saddens me a little to think
                that thousands of generations of us
                devoted cockroaches are left in the lurch
                but the fact is that the legit stage
```

is no longer the theater in a big way
the moving picture is the theater now
the living and real theater

archy flies

well boss i have had
some experiences you know that
fellow with the teeth that glitter
and the eyes that glitter who
comes in to see you and
who has been talking about his aeroplane
for six months you thought he
was always a liar and
so did i he is the kind of a liar who
looks so much like a liar no one
believes him when he tells the
truth i thought i would call
his bluff so i crawled into
his outside breast pocket the other day
and went out to a place near mineola
with him he really has an aeroplane he
went up in it the next morning and
i went along boss i must have
picked out the wrong position i sat
on top of one of the planes thinking i would see
more of the country boss
dont ask me for any sensations the
only thing i felt was wind i felt
like a sigh in a cyclone i had
about as much control of myself as a
bullet that is going through the
barrel of an airgun i dont want
to rub anything in boss but it
was as hard to hang onto as the water
wagon which is a simile
you may be able to appreciate i

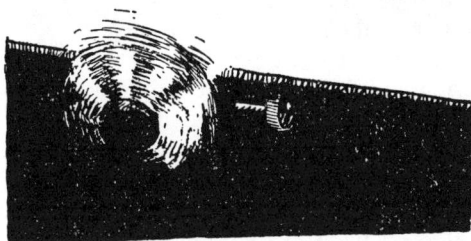

i must have picked out the wrong position

dug all my feet and claws
and teeth in but the wind rushed by
me like a church scandal going
through a little village i would have
felt nausea if
my stomach hadnt been scared to death
it was only a question of time before i
would let loose thank heaven i thought i am
not an elephant i didnt
want to die again so soon just because
i can come to life again is
no reason for overworking a good thing too
many deaths and transmigrations look

vulgar and ostentatious
and when i did let go i must have
been two miles high around and
around i spun whirling like a flake of
soot that has been flipped
off of a devils wing between the
worlds and is spinning back home to
hell and beneath me it looked
like hell there was a vast expanse of water
with the sun making it
seem like melted metal i suppose i said
i will get all my feet wet now and
take my death of cold if a fish
dont eat me and just then i saw
beneath me a great fish grinning as if
he had heard a joke on the
bottom of the sea and come up to
laugh at the cosmos get that
cosmic stuff boss it goes great in some
circles i lit on one of his great white teeth
and waited for the gulp that should land
me in his interior department oh
lord i said if i ever see dry land i
will never mock at that jonah story
again i dont want to die in
midocean and be reincarnated as a
sardine or as an oyster
a cockroach isnt much but
he has a look in in society where
an oyster is never mentioned except as an
article of food but if it
must be it must be kismet and karma and
that bunch of bullies vote us the way they
please we are only instructed delegates
in the universal convention every
time i die it makes me more of a fatalist and
i waited for him to gulp but
he didnt gulp i hopped over to
the next tooth to the right as you go in
and investigated and finally climbed

out where his upper lip would have been if he had
had one and worked up to his eye it was
glassy in death i was floating on a dead shark
and it was all the more unpleasant
because he had not had any dental work done for a
long time or else he had adenoids or maybe
he had died of ptomaine poisoning boss what i am
delicately trying to convey is
that he had been dead so long he had a right to
be ashamed of it just then i
heard human voices and looking around i saw
two young men in bathing suits and
a motor boat a shark a shark cried one
of them put her about the motor is still
busted said the other row row for your
life but wait said the first one this
shark seems deceased bill lets haul him to land
and say we slew him right o tom says
bill it will make a hit with all the girls he
attacked us says tom and i jumped into the water and
cut his throat with my jackknife you
did eh says bill what was i doing then put two
slashes into him which they did one for each and
fastened him to the stern of their boat with a
line and as they towed him to the beach with
me sitting listening they fixed
up an awful lie talk about ovations boss when they
came to the beach they got one the
more i see of human nature the less i know
whether to despise it for being so easily
gulled or for being so ready to
gull by the time they had told
that story eight times each believed that
he was telling the truth although he
still thought maybe the other one was lying well
i left those two heroes
surrounded six deep by girls and came to
town in a little bunch of dress goods samples a
commuters wife has been trying to make
him remember to match my

[379]

sympathies being with the shark poor feeble **old**
thing he had likely perished of old age
to be killed a second time is hard luck but
this is the truth of a story that you
may read another version of in
the news columns

archy

archy and the suicide

well boss i have just
been assisting at a suicide i think the
gentleman who killed himself was
quite right in doing so too
i went into the kitchen of an
up town hotel the other
evening for a bite to eat and after
i had dined i thought
i would look the place over and if
i found a room that appealed to me i
would spend the night there
the room i got into was already
infested by a little old bald headed fellow
with scared eyes and a face like
a petrified turnip who was
hunched up under a reading lamp
reading a
bible all of a sudden he gave a
jump and said gawd gawd there it
is again and i saw a puff of
smoke floating across the
table in front of him it seemed to come
from nowhere in particular smoke
smoke cried the old man i am
haunted by smoke and as
he spoke another puff of smoke
suddenly appeared from nowhere on
the table in front of him

gawd gawd he cried spare me spare
me do not persecute me this way
and i will give all the money to charity
i will give it to the red
cross or any church you
may designate i know
i did wrong to burn down that
building for the
insurance money but how was i
to know there was any one in it i
did not plan a murder a third
puff of smoke seemed to start out of
his own shoulder and floated in
front of his eyes and a fourth
puff hit him on his bald head and made
a little veil in front of his face
gawd gawd he cried and threw
himself on the rug and began to
pray with his face hidden i
thought to myself those
puffs of smoke are peculiar there
isnt anything on fire in
here and then i got a whiff of it
and it smelled like tobacco smoke
then i saw something that looked
like a gray globe floating from the
direction of the bathroom door it
drifted across the room and hit
the reading lamp and vanished with a
puff of smoke i looked at the
bathroom door and i thought i
heard some one chuckle over there and
then i saw another gray globe of smoke forming
at the keyhole it slowly grew and grew till it
was as big as a baseball and then it
detached itself from the door and
floated across the room
i crawled noiselessly under the bath
room door it was one of those bath
rooms midway between two sleeping

rooms and there were a couple of
chuckle headed young fellows sitting
on the floor laughing to
themselves both were about half
soused and they were having a good
time one of them had a slender hollow
brass curtain rod and he was soaping
the end of it and
sticking it into the keyhole then he
would fill his mouth with cigarette
smoke and blow a soap bubble which
drifted into the old mans room what
is he doing now said one of them he
is on the floor praying said the
other taking the rod out of the
keyhole and looking through let me
blow a couple said the first young
man you are too soused said the
second one dont be selfish said the
first one gawd gawd said the voice
from the room i had just left i am
haunted by ghostly smoke i will live
right all the rest of my life if you
only let me off this time
give him another bubble said the
first young man he has got it
coming to him evidently so
they gave him half a dozen more
bubbles the noise
in the haunted mans room ceased for
some minutes what is he doing now
said the first young man i cant see
him said the second one just then
there came a kicking kind of a noise
on the wall i went into the
haunted mans room and found his
closet door was open i went in and he
was just dying he had hanged himself
to a hook on the wall with a trunk
cord those two young fellows had

just the wrong man for their little
practical joke or
just the right man if you want to
look at it that way i
went away from there at once not
wishing to be on hand if there
was any investigation yours
for conscience and coincidence
and may they never meet

archy

and found out too late

comforting thoughts

a fish who had
swallowed an angle worm
found all too late
that a hook was nesting
in its midst ah me
said the poor fish
i am the most luckless
creature in the world
had you not pointed
that out said the worm
i might have supposed

[384]

myself a trifle
unfortunate
cheer up you two said
the fisherman jovially
the first two minutes
of that hook are always
the worst you must
cultivate a philosophic
state of mind
boss there is always
a comforting thought
in time of trouble when
it is not our trouble

                              archy '

inspiration

excuse me if my
writing is out of alignment i
fell into a bowl of
egg nog the other
day at the restaurant down
the street which the doctor
says he is glad to
hear you are keeping away
from and when i
emerged i was full of happy
inspirations alas they
vanished ere the break of
day i am sure they
were the most brilliant and
witty things that ever
emanated from the mind of
man or cockroach or poet i
sat inside a mince pie
and laughed and laughed at
them myself the world seemed all
one golden glory boss

i came up the
street to get all this
wonderful stuff onto paper for
you but when i tried to
operate the typewriter
my foot would slip and
by the time i had control
of the machine again
the thoughts had gone
forever it is the
tragedy of the artist

                              archy

gossip

well boss it is
surprising how many
gossips there are left in
this world and how
easy it is to ruin a
person s reputation
a few days ago an
alleged friend of yours
remarked to another
alleged friend i saw
archy on a bun in
a cafe down town the other
day and the second alleged
friend told another person
that archy had been seen
publicly intoxicated and
the other person went
around saying poor
archy he drinks like a
water bug until my
reputation is ruined you
would think i was
the habitual companion of

the well known dipsas snake
and the truth of
the whole thing is very
simple your alleged friend did
see me on a bun
in a cafe it was a
common ordinary bun such as
you spread butter on
and eat and i
was eating at it
just as i would sit on any other
piece of bread and eat but
now all my friends are
saying to me
did i see you on a
bun or did i not
answer yes or no and if i
answer no they say
prevaricator i saw you on a
bun and if i answer yes they
say i thought so and
will not let me explain and
if i do not answer
at all they say
aha too full for
utterance sometimes i
hate the world

                    archy

a close call

thank you boss for the
swiss cheese i hardly hoped
for a whole one i
took up quarters in it at once
the little galleries and caves and
runways appealed to
my sense of adventure after
i had made a square
meal i lay down in the inner
chamber for a nap feeling
safe i had hardly composed my limbs
for slumber when i heard
a gnawing sound and squeaks
of glee cautiously i
approached the north gallery a mouse
was there i hastily
retreated thinking i would make
my escape by way of one of the
windows on the south facade another
mouse was there the citadel
in short was attacked on all sides mice
mice mice coming nearer and nearer
their cold blooded squeaks and the champing
of their cruel teeth made the night
hideous minute after minute i lay
in the stokehold
until the slow minutes grew into
intolerable hours of agony great drops
of perspiration broke through the callus
on my brow i prayed for
dawn or the night watchman suddenly
into my retreat protruded a whisker it
was so near it tickled me closer and
closer it came it twitched i knew
that it had felt me a moment more and

all would be over just as
i prepared myself for another
transmigration mehitabel the cat
bounded into the room and i was saved
if you get me another cheese please
put a wire cage over it

archy

kidding the boss

well boss if i
were you i would not
put too much
trust in the
candor of those people
who tell you that you
will ever learn to
play kelley pool a
cockroach who lives
in one of the
pockets of the
pool table of that place
where you are so
often inveigled into playing
tells me that he
has never yet had to
dodge a ball that
you hit he sticks his
head out of his dugout
and watches the
game in perfect security
while you are shooting he
says it is a shame
the way you fall for the
flattery of those who
tell you that you are
improving my only
interest in the

matter is connected
with the fact that if
you wasted less
money on what will
always remain a game of
chance to you
you might be able to
do the square thing by
me and slip a
little money my way
now and then
for my contributions

                              archy

a sermon

well boss here
we are on the job again
you simply cannot
keep a good bug down
as a cockroach friend
of mine once
remarked to a fat man
who had
inadvertently
swallowed him along
with a portion
of hungarian goulash
although the remark
i understand
originated with jonah
well the main
thing is to keep
cheerful in spite
of the ups and
downs as i
heard an oyster
remark to his mate

last evening
only six weeks till
may says he
and if we go that long
without being eaten
we will get through
till september and
maybe by that time
nobody will want to
eat us no such
luck for us says
she nonsense says
he be more optimistic
i have noticed
every year that if
i get through
march i always
get through the rest
of the year
and just at that
moment a waiter
put the melancholy
oyster on a plate to
be served and eaten
and rejected the
cheerful oyster
there is a great
moral lesson
in this i pick
up a great many
little sermons of this
sort in my capacity as a
roach about town

                         archy

difficulties of art

boss why dont you get a
ribbon put into your typewriter it is only
after the most desperate exertions that
i am able to pound out these few lines i
had to get a sheet of carbon paper
and insert it between two sheets of white paper
and fix it in the machine in order to
write at all and would never have got it
done if it hadnt been that mehitabel the
cat and all the rest of the gang
around here helped me i had something
important i wanted to write you but all this
frightful physical labor has driven it out
of my mind it is always so with the
artist by the time he has overcome the
difficulties that lie between him and
his masterpiece
he is tired i wish you would get me an
electric typewriter and why not have me
endowed so i would not have to worry about
material things at all i would like to write
and eat and sleep and not work at anything else

archy

We said to Archy the other day: "You are welcome to
our house any time you wish, if you come alone. But
please cease bringing your friends and kinsfolk with
you." To which he replied:

boss
you should have learned
by this time
that literature
   makes strange
bedfellows

the captain s little golden headed daughter
flung crumbs to the hungry porpoises

a spiggoty hero

i met a big spiggoty cockroach
down by one of the
docks where the fruit steamships come in
the other day who says he
is quite a hero
the deed he did will soon be
shown in the movies he thinks for
he is certain that a camera
man was present
an american battleship was going through

one of the locks of the
panama canal he says and
the captain s little golden
headed daughter was sitting in the
bows flinging crumbs from a sea
biscuit to the hungry porpoises
which flocked about the vessel when
in hurling a large crumb she lost her
balance and fell overboard the
old lock keeper immediately became rattled the
ship was half way through the gate when
the child fell among the
porpoises and the old lock keeper
saw her fall and let
loose of the lever
the ponderous gates were swinging shut and
both the battleship and the
little golden haired girl would
have been caught between them and
pinched into nothingness if
this spiggoty cockroach
according to his story had not retained his
presence of mind
he gave one leap he says and landed
on one of the cog wheels that
are worked by the old lock keeper s lever
he braced himself between a cog on one
wheel and a cog on the other and
exerted all his strength and in
an instant the machinery was stopped because
the wheels could no longer revolve he
made himself a wedge he says
it was a great strain he says and the
pressure on his forehead and feet was
something frightful the old lock keeper
plunged in among the porpoises and handed up
the little golden haired girl
to the ship and just then the captain of
the vessel noticed that the
heroic cockroach was weakening and hastily

sent a cabin boy to find a
bootjack which when found
he inserted among the cogs thus
releasing the heroic cockroach who fell
unconscious to the deck of the vessel the
old lock keeper returned to his duty grasped the
lever again and the bootjack was
removed the ship sailing onward happy
and safe the captain insisted on decorating
him in front of the crew for his
heroism he would have shown me the decorations
he said but on his way north he
was very hungry and ate them up
in his sleep one night he dreamed he
was eating he says and when he woke at
dawn he found the decorations had
disappeared but he did show me the scars
on his forehead and feet to
prove his story i will not say there
was rum on the ship that he came north on but
i will say that there was
something that did not smell quite like
molasses on his breath as he talked to me and i
should like to see the movie
films before i underwrite the story i told
him so and he acted sad and
injured if i had been lying he said i
could have thought of a better lie than
that something more picturesque i would have
said that the old lock keepers whiskers got caught
in the cog wheels and he was
being slowly drawn into the
machinery and would have
died a horrible death and that i
rescued him as well as the little
girl and the battleship well we went
down the street and met another
roach a friend of mine and this
spiggoty told the story to him and when he
told it he said that the old

lock keepers whiskers had been caught and
so forth
and showed a gray horsehair he had
picked up on the street a moment before and
said it was a hair from the old
lock keepers beard which he
had given him as a keepsake in
vino veritas may be right but rum if
it was rum i smelled seems to work
differently

                                    archy

sociological

when the cold weather
comes i always
get a new interest in sociology
i am almost human that way
it worries me as to how
the other half
are going to get through
the winter
last evening i went
into a cheap eating house
and dropped into a beef stew
and had a warm bath
and a bite to eat
and listened afterwards
to a couple of bums
who had begged enough
during the day to get a supper
they were talking
about this new movement
on the part of the jobless
and homeless
to take possession of the churches
and live there during
the cold weather

said the first bum
i dont think i could do it
it would bring up
too many associations
you see i am a minister s son
you too exclaimed the second bum
why i also
am the son of a preacher
my father was a minister
in small towns all his life
he worked himself to death at it
he never got paid enough
to live on
and it was not until i left home
and became a hobo that i ever
got as much as i wanted to eat
at one meal
precisely my experience
said the other bum
have you ever had any temptation
said number one
to quit being a hobo
and take a regular job
yes said number two
very often
but i have always had
the strength of character
to resist temptation
it is my duty to my fellow men
to see that they have
material on which to wreak
their passion to be charitable
during the christmas holidays
it makes the well to do
more comfortable and gives
them a warm virtuous glow
when they give me a dime
and i should not feel justified
in taking from them
such a simple and inexpensive pleasure

yes said the other bum
the rich we have always with us
they are the great problem of the age
we must treat them as well
as we can and help them
to have a little fun by the way
so that they can forget
at least temporarily
the biblical assurance
that it is as hard for them to enter
the kingdom of heaven
as for a camel
to pass through a needle s eye
well said the other one
sometimes i think i would
be willing to change places
with a rich man
and run the risk
oh certainly said the other
i have never had any instinctive
hatred for riches
it is only work that i detest
riches are all very well
if you inherit them
but i doubt if they are worth
toiling for
think of all the millions
toiling miserably in order
to be damned
it is a pathetic sight
but if one inherits riches
he knows that the fates
have doomed him to be damned
before his birth
and it is of little use to struggle
that is far different from striving
desperately all one s life
to lay up enough wealth
to damn one
i perceive said his new found friend

that your early training
has stayed by you
you have a truly religious nature
yes replied the other
at the cost of great
personal sacrifice in many ways
i have kept myself
an object of charity
in order to foster
the spirituality of the well to do
the most passionate piety
could do but little more
but if you had inherited
great riches said the other bum
would you have given them to the poor
i doubt was the reply
that i would have felt justified
in doing that
i would more likely have said to myself
that providence
had by that token
marked me out as one destined
to hell fire
and i would have considered it
impious to struggle against
the manifest wishes of heaven
well sighed the other
life is full of terrible problems
indeed it is
rejoined his friend
but i am afraid that i shall
never solve even the least of them
when i am empty and cold
i am not in the mood for meditation
and when i am warm and replete
i go to sleep
the few guiding principles
i learned in father s church
have carried me thus far
and i shall go on to the end

[399]

never thinking beyond them
i merely apply them literally
and they work
they have made me what i am
he concluded complacently

archy

never blame the booze

as i go up and down the town
hither to and fro i gather many a
smile and frown and talk of
thus and so i lately
listened and i heard two chaps
their luck bewail life did not get
a pleasant word they
told an awful tale for one of them
had just been fired he
glummed and wondered why he cried
into his beer
aspired
to punch the boss his eye too
true the other one exclaimed this
world s a burning shame the
game of living has been framed it is
a rotten game and ever as they railed
at fate and wooed the sombre muse
they steadily absorbed a great
sufficiency of booze but neither one
that cursed his luck and beat his burning bean
would blame the downfall on the truck
that passed his lips between
and as i listened there i thought it were
more candid far to give its dues to what they bought
across the varnished bar they should indeed
be far more frank about their hard lucks boss
they should remark
each genial tank unto their bosses faces

you can t expect a man to drink as much as i do boss
and have much time to work and think
and put the job across
oh boss you ask too much of me
i do the best i can but who can lush
continually and be a working man
you can t expect a man to booze from morning
until night and feel quite nimble
in his shoes and add his figures right oh boss
you ask too much of us we have no flair for toil
we d rather daily dally thus imbibing joyful oil
you can t expect a man to souse
and do work for your business house so do not be
    unjust
twere more like reason if they said such words
unto their bosses than tear the hair
and beat the head and blame luck
for their losses

                                archy

the sad crickets

well boss it may
surprise you to learn
that a cricket does not
sing to be cheerful
as chas dickens believed
he sings because he
feels so melancholy i
asked one with whom
i have become well
acquainted what his song
meant and he
replied
there are no words
to go with
that music but the
music is sad i

[401]

make that music these
hot nights because i
have prickly heat
and there is nothing else
to do and another
cricket said yes
our song is sad i am
not troubled by the
heat but my song is
melancholy too the words to
my song said the second
cricket are as follows
and he repeated them for
me to wit
my love fell into a spiders web
squeak squeak squeak
and she screamed with pain as he
crunched her bones into his
bloody beak squeak squeak
squeak yes i said that is
sad very sad said the
cricket but not as sad as the
second stanza which goes
as follows my love got caught in
the crack of the door squeak
squeak squeak and i think with
grief of the way she died whenever
i hear it creak
squeak squeak squeak
whenever i hear it creak
squeak squeak squeak
that brings tears to my eyes
i said yes he said
there is nothing you could call
jolly about the
second stanza nor the
third fourth and fifth stanzas
friend i said
hurriedly let me hear the
last stanza

he looked at me as if
i had struck him
and hurried off with
tears in his gentle eyes
one thing that
makes crickets so
melancholy is that
they have the artistic
temperament

archy

fond recollections

boss i saw a
pitiful sight yesterday i
was crawling across the
ruins of an old house that
the workmen are tearing
down up town and
i saw a middle
aged man sitting on a
pile of bricks with
his gray hair in his hands he
was weeping and moaning
and i gathered from his
remarks that the place was once
a boarding house where
he had spent
many happy years i caught
a few strophes of his
song of woe as
follows
o workman spare that bathtub o
that bathtub made of zinc
that bathtub in the boarding house
that i lived in for years
fond recollections of
my youth surge oer

me when i think
upon that bathtub in that
boarding house and i
choke up with tears
when splashing of a sunday
morn a peevish voice and surly
would tell me to make
haste and be
myself again adorning
throughout the week it
had few friends
but o on sunday morning
that bathtub in the
boarding house was
busy bright and early
how well i can remember how
as i tripped down the hall
the boarders heads would
be poked out along the
corridor
the sound of some one singing
upon my ears would fall
and sounds of others waiting
and getting very sore
o workman spare that
bathtub to me it does
bring back
the merry days when i was
young and all the world was pink
o workman spare that bathtub
from ruin and from rack
the bathtub in the
boarding house
the bathtub made of zinc

                                    archy

immorality

i was up to central
park yesterday watching some
kids build a snow man when
they were done and had
gone away i looked it
over they had used two
little chunks of wood for
the eyes i sat on one
of these and stared at
the bystanders along came a
prudish looking
lady from flatbush she
stopped and regarded the
snow man i stood
up on my hind legs in
the eye socket and
waved myself at her
horrors she cried even the
snow men in manhattan
are immoral officer arrest
that statue it winked
at me madam said the cop
accept the tribute
as a christmas present
and be happy my own
belief is that some
people have immorality
on the brain

archy

archy is excited

dear boss i am
acquiring more
and more contempt
for you humans
i heard a couple
of girls yesterday
saying what a nice
christmas present it
would make to catch
a live archy
and have him gilded and
wear him on
a little chain
attached to a scarf
pin yours for red rum
ruin revolt and rapine

archy

archy reports

ive got just one
resolution for this year boss
and here it is
better stuff and more rhymes
what have i got to look
forward to otherwise if
a vers libre poet is
reincarnated into
a cockroach what will
a vers libre cockroach
be reincarnated into i
ask you
i don t want to be

a amoeba next time do i
i sing the glad noo year
thats tending toward the norm
my song is one of cheer
im going to reform
see

                              archy

archy says

i suppose the human race
is doing the best it can
but hells bells thats
only an explanation
its not an excuse

i heard a dry telling a flapper
the other day that since repeal
the women are drinking
too much gin
and the young lady
thoughtfully replied o nerts
there aint too much gin
there aint hardly enough

mehitabel the cat
was running around with a tom cat
off a cruiser when the fleet
was in new york
and she said to me yesterday
archy i wish you would come
down to shinbone alley
and see the seven funny little
sea serpents yowling around there
trying to put it across on me
that i am their parent
every time i go in for
a platonic friendship

[407]

there aint too much gin
there aint hardly enough

it turns out plutonic
my maternal instinct
has proved to be a great drawback
it started when i was practically
a debutante and has been going
from bad to worse ever since

my ideals are putty
your ikons made of mud
and so you think me nutty
and i think youre a dud

                              archy

[408]

the book worm

well boss i had one gay
time last night i ran
onto a book worm in one of
the tomes on your desk and
found him a friendly
little cuss come he said to
me with his little eyes
shining brightly through his
horn rimmed glasses let us
make a night of it let us
have a gay evening lead on
says i we will go says
he to the annual
exhibit of the new york
microscopical society at the
american museum of natural
history they have there
some treponema pallidum some
models of amoeba and
paramoecium and some
pediculus capitis the deuce you
say said i yes said he it
will be a rare treat
indeed there are also some
ziroons there showing their
pioochroic halos the
nerve of them i said do
the authorities know it my
word yes says he the department of
health is responsible for
it come let us hasten there is
also a fine selection
of diplococci to say nothing
of the protococcus nivalls and
a specimen of phlogopito
from canada it sounds like a

jolly gang i said will there
be anything to drink
at this party i understand
he said that cerebro spinal
fluid will flow
like water the gay dogs i
said guide me to
it professor its always
fair weather when good fellows get
together i must warn
you he says that one
is not allowed to feed the
animalculae well when we
got there what do you
suppose the bunch was
germs boss germs just
ordinary germs pardon me i said
i will associate
with insects humans and
ghosts but not knowingly
with germs you must excuse me
one must draw the line somewhere
these friends of yours look
like alien enemies to me they
may have noble names but
their blood is thin
so i left
him flat and dropped into
a beef steak pie in one
of these arm chair restaurants for
a bite to eat and a
warm bath before
going to bed
that book worm was
out for some wild
evening boss its strange how
many of these quiet
looking little high brows have
bohemian tastes

archy

i rode on it that s how i got back here

archy s comet

several persons have
asked me during
the last few days have
you seen the comet
and my answer has been
seen it why
i rode on it
that is how i got
back here after my
travels it is my private
comet i park

it up there and it
waits until i am ready
to go somewhere
else ask me something
different

                              archy

progress

if mars
and earth ever do
get into communication
probably they will be
swapping
scandalous stories
inside of three hours

                              archy

he has enemies

boss i dont want to
be importunate or nag you or
anything like that but
working nights and sleeping by day as
much as i do i dont get
time to hustle up any
grub for myself wont
you please leave
something behind the radiator it has
been three days since i ate i might
have dined on an apple core last night
but there was white powder
sprinkled near it and over it i
have my enemies boss a little scrap of
dried beef would be appreciated

                              archy

barbarous

in a restaurant uptown
i dropped into a beef stew
yesterday for a warm bath
and a bite to eat
and i heard a horrid discussion
between a waiter and a customer
they were talking about fishing
and the customer says the best luck
he ever had was one time when he
was staying at a run down hotel
in the country and he used cockroaches for bait
the waiter made a note
and says he is going to write
to a rod and gun column in a paper about it
yes says the customer do so and i bet you
in a year from now
they won t be using anything but cockroaches
and they will be worth almost
their weight in gold
boss please petition congress at once
and get a law passed
against cruel and unusual bait
after all i have done for this country
am i to be in danger
of getting the hook like that
if you abolish the cockroaches
no boarding house will seem like home
and no home like a boarding house
why i have lived in places
which would have fallen down
if the spider webs and cockroaches
had been removed
i consider fishing a barbarous sport anyhow
                                        archy

pulled a piece of cheese rind over my head

the demon rum

well boss on these
rainy days i wish i was
web footed like a jersey mosquito no
one has yet invented
an umbrella for cockroaches i was
over across the street
to the barroom you used to
frequent before you reformed today
and it was raining outside i
pulled a piece of cheese

rind over my head to
protect me from the weather and
started for the door as i
passed by one of the booths a man
who was sitting in it said to
his companion please call a
taxi for me where do you want to go
said his companion i am
bad again said the man i want to
go to some place where they
treat nervous diseases
at once you look all right
said his companion i may look all
right said he but i don t see
all right i just saw a piece
of cheese rind crawling along the
floor and as i passed by i
said to myself beware the demon rum
it gives your brain a quirk
it puts you on the bum
and gives the doctors work

                                        archy

ancient lineage

professor slosson
says that the cockroach
is one of the eldest of the
creatures that inhabit
the globe
two hundred and fifty
millions of years
ago the cockroach
existed just as he exists
today of course it is
very flattering
to have this scientific
testimony to my ancient

[415]

lineage i can trace my
ancestry back without
a break to old adam cockroach
himself but the real question is
how much has the cockroach
learned in two hundred and
fifty million of years
well i can tell you
in a few brief words
the cockroach has learned
how to make man
the so called lord
of creation work for him
the cockroach lives
in peace and plenty
while the human race
hustles to support him
all the social institutions
of all time have existed
merely for the purpose
of forming a pyramid
on the apex of which
perches the cockroach triumphant
it has taken us a long
time but we point
with pride to the achievement
if you don t believe me
read professor slosson s
article

                    archy

quaint

"Does Archy ever visit Greenwich Village?" asks **R.P.** "I found myself in company with a cockroach of a dissipated but still scholarly appearance in one of the cafés over there the other evening. . . ."

Archy, we regret to say, will frequent the Village. Indeed, we hear that he is planning to open a café of his own to be known as "Ye Crusty Cockroach."

"But why the 'Ye,' Archy?" we asked him. "Why not merely 'The'?"

And Archy, loping six-leggedly to the typewriter, laboriously replied:

it is going to be one
of those quaint
places boss and all those
quaint places have to
be ye instead of the
in a ye place you can
serve almost anything
and get away
with it but in a
the place you have to
have a certain amount
of eats and drinks
and that increases the
expense of operation
enormously i am no
pig but i do wish to
make enough money once in
my life to be
among the
excess prophets or the
excise profits or
what ever you call
them

For our part, we shall never eat goulash in a place
that is conducted by Archy—so many of these Greenwich Village artists are always Putting Themselves Into
Their Work.

the artist

i called on some friends in a
studio building the other evening and
while we were foraging about
for something to eat
we got caught on a
palette smeared over with all
the colors there are
leaping from this danger seven
or eight of us
landed upon an untouched canvas
that stood upon an easel
nearby waiting for the masters hand
and we walked across the
canvas on our way out of that
place it seems that we builded
better than we knew before
we could get to any safer place
than a spot behind a
gas radiator we heard human footsteps
approaching and an
instant later two men entered the
studio one of them switched on
the lights and the
other gave an exclamation of
pleasure and astonishment by jove
tommy he said to the owner of
the studio what is this new thing
of yours on the easel it is
the best thing you have done yet
i thought you were against
modernism and all

the new fangled stuff but i see
that you have come over to the new
school your style has
loosened up wonderfully old kid
i always said that if you
could only get away from the stiffness
and absurdity of the
conventional schools you had the
makings of a great painter in
you what do you call this
picture tommy
well said tommy with rare
presence of mind i have not
named it yet it is not altogether in
the newer mode you will observe i
have been struggling for a
compromise between the two methods
that would at the same time
allow me to express my
individuality on canvas i do
think myself that i have got more
freshness and directness into this
thing you have said his friend
it has the direct and naive approach
of the primitives and it
also has all that is
worthy to be retained of the
reticent sophistication of
the post pre raphaelites but what
do you say you are going to
call it it is said tommy as
you see a nocturne i have
been thinking of calling it
impressions of brooklyn
bridge in a fog and when his
friend went out he stood and looked at
the picture for a long time and
said now i wonder who in
hell slipped in here and did that it
is nothing short of genius could

i have done it myself when i
was drunk i must have done so
anyhow i will sign it and
taking up a brush he did so well i
stole a look at the canvas
myself and it looked like nothing
on earth to me but a canvas over
which a lot of cockroaches had
walked i may be a
critic but still i know what i
dont like yours for another
renaissance of the arts every
spring and every autumn

                                        archy

the suicide club

boss i ran onto a queer bunch
in the back room of a saloon on william street
the other night there were six of them
two cockroaches
a grass hopper
a flea
and two crickets
they have what they call a suicide club
not the sort our old
friend r l s made famous
the members of which intend to kill
themselves but each member of this
club has committed suicide already
they were once humans
as i was myself
at least i was a poet
after they killed themselves their souls
transmigrated into the bodies
of the insects mentioned
and so they have got together and
formed a club the other night the grass

just as i got my shoe off
we passed a glue factory

hopper told why he had killed himself
it was a misunderstanding
with one i loved he said
which impelled me to the rash act
she and i were walking down a country
road and i got some gravel in one
of my shoes shortly afterward we
boarded a trolley car would you
mind i asked her if i took my shoe off
and shook out the gravel
help yourself she said
just as i got my shoe off we passed
a glue factory
i hastily put the shoe on again by the

time it was on again we were well past
the glue factory
the period during which the shoe was off
and the period during which we
were passing the glue factory exactly
synchronized
she did not see the glue factory
and refused to believe there had been
one in the neighborhood i could
never explain a month later
i killed myself tough luck
old top said the flea i will now
tell you why i took the fatal
plunge i will
tell you how it was i
committed suicide and transmigrated
into the body of an insect i was
the india rubber man in a circus side
show and fell in love with a
pair of beautiful siamese twins
public opinion was against
me marrying both of them
although both of them loved me as i
loved them both you
must choose between them said the
manager what god has joined together
let no man put asunder i said but
public opinion was too much for me
but the surgical operation which
severed them changed their
dispositions you cant fool with
a freak without running some such
risk when they were cut apart one of
them eloped with the surgeon
who had done the work and the other
married an interne in the
hospital they had a double
wedding and i slew myself that night
well said one of the crickets i will
now tell you how i shuffled off

this mortal coil and
transmigrated into the
body of a cricket and became a
member of this has been club my father
belonged to a religious sect which
forbids shaving and i was
brought up in that way no
razor ever touched my face when i was
forty years old i had a beard that hung
down to my knees it was red and
glossy i went around the country
posing as a doctor for a medicine
company hitting the tank towns in a
wagon and giving a spiel and
playing on the banjo i did well as
my beard attracted
crowds and was happy and
prosperous until one day a
malignant old man who
had just bought six bottles of tonic
for five dollars made of roots herbs
and natures own remedies
containing no
mineral ingredients and brewed from
juniper leaves hazel roots choke
cherries and the bark of the
wild cohosh exactly
as the indians made it for a
thousand years
in the unpathed forests before the
pale face came said to me mister
can i ask you a question yes i
said i have nothing to conceal i am on
the level if one wine glass full before
meals does not give you an appetite
take two or three
mister he says the question is
personal go ahead i says i am the
seventh son
of a seventh son a soothsayer and a

seer i can tell by the way
you chew tobacco you have liver
trouble i will make a
special price to you fourteen
bottles for ten dollars cash no he said
it is about your beard it grew i told
him through using this medicine
my chin was bald at
birth it is a specific for erysipelas
botts neuralgia stomach trouble loss
of appetite hearts disease dandruff and
falling hair thirty bottles to you
for twenty dollars and i will throw
in an electric belt
mister he said i only want to ask
you if you sleep
with all your beard outside
of the covers or
under the covers when you go to
bed at night and he gave me an evil
grin and went on i
never thought of it
before i had just gone to bed and slept
as a rule but that night when i
climbed into bed i thought of the old
mans question i spread all my
beard outside of the covers and it
was immediately apparent to me
that i did not have the habit of
sleeping with it that way then i put it
under the covers and was
no less certain that i did not
sleep with it that way i worried
about it till morning and each way i
put it seemed at
once to be the wrong way
the next night it was the same
thing i could not keep from
thinking about it i got no sleep at all
and became the mere shadow of my

former self it so preyed upon me
that at last i saw i must either
shave off the beard or end it all but i
could not shave off the beard
without deserting the religious principles
instilled into me by my father and so i
took the fatal plunge hard lines said the
second cricket the way i happened to
commit suicide and undergo
transmigration and
thus qualify for a member of this club
was this when i was a
human i was wedded to a lady whose
mother had a very strong
and domineering character she
lived with us night after
night i would lie awake thinking
up schemes to get even
with her i thought up
some lovely schemes but when
morning came my nerve would
leave i never had the courage to
put them into execution finally
the thought came to me that if i was
a ghost i could haunt her and
she would have no come back i slew
myself but alas my soul transmigrated
into the body of a cricket and
if you had ever seen that strong and
bitter old woman slaying spiders and
crickets you could realize
the despair that has settled down on me
since too bad said one
of the cockroaches i will now narrate the
events which led up to my
determination to
take the leap into the
darkness
i cant say that i
had any good reason for

slaying myself i had done everything
else at least once i was a
young man possessed of a
considerable fortune which it was my only
occupation to dissipate when
everything else palled i
took up theology i made a bet
with another student that the soul
was not immortal the only way to
settle it was to die and find out we both
did well fellows we both lost mine
proved to be immortal for here i am but his
was not it completely disappeared and
has never been heard of again
which shows you never can tell and
yet i am still interested in
games of chance

                                        archy

psychic

boss i have had a terrible time
since i last wrote you as i
told you long ago i was originally a
vers libre poet and my
soul after leaving that body
migrated into the
body of a cockroach before that
happened i did not believe in the
doctrine of transmigration of
souls but after it happened
how could i refuse to credit it well
it gave me a great deal of interest
in all psychic matters and it
struck me not many weeks ago that
if it were possible for a soul
to leave a poet that way and go into
the body of a cockroach
at the poets death it might be
possible to manage it without death the
truth is that i got tired of being a
cockroach and wanted to be
human again i practised and practised
until i found myself able to get out
of the cockroach body and
naked on the air of heaven ride but it
is not all that it is cracked up to be
there is nothing that can get so
cold as a soul these autumn nights
when it has no body and no blankets
and in winter it is worse yet after i
had gained proficiency i began
to look around for a human to
get into but as far as i could
learn every human was filled with
a soul already but i began to
make longer and longer trips away from
my cockroach body imagine my

consternation and surprise one day
some weeks ago upon returning to the
cockroach body which i had left to find
that it had been squashed and swept out
with a broom i looked at the fragments
with horror it was a very discouraged
looking set of remains but there i
was out in the world with
no shelter all sould up as you might
say and no place to go it may strike you
as nothing to worry about and it
wasnt so bad for a day or two but there
is a horrid sense of helplessness
about it if you are interested in
psychic research and that
sort of thing you can get a
little fun for a while appearing in
seances and balling up the messages
but believe me psychic research is more
interesting when you are the human calling
up the spirits than when you
are the ghost too often
they make you the goat that
soon palled on me and i wandered for
weeks the most lonely thing in new york
city at last in despair i
got into the carcase of another cockroach
again of about the same size and
general appearance of my old frame but
the whole affair has had a most
depressing effect on me imagine taking
all that trouble to get away from
being a cockroach and then get
shoved back into one by
fate again i think i will
stick to the old homestead for a
while how do i know but what the next
time i might get into the body of a
flea or a communist

archy

destiny

well boss here i
am a cockroach still boss
i have often been disgusted
with life but now i am
even more disgusted
with death and transmigration i
would rather not inhabit
any body at all than
inhabit a cockroachs
body but it seems i
cant escape it that
is my destiny my doom my
punishment
when you struck me that
terrific blow a few
days ago and i
died there at
your feet my first
sensation was one of glad
relief what body will
the soul of archy transmigrate
into now i asked
myself will i go
higher in the scale of
life and inhabit the
body of a butterfly
or a dog or a
bird or will i sink
lower and go into the
carcase of a poison
spider or a politician
i sat on a blade of
grass and waited and wondered
what it would be i
hoped it wouldnt be

anything at all too soon
because if you remember
it was a hot
day and as i sat
on that blade of grass
in my naked soul and
let my feet hang over i
was deliciously
cool try it some of
these hot nights leave
your body in the
bed and go up on the
roof in your
spirit and float around
like a toy balloon its
great stuff well while
i was sitting there
thinking what i
would inhabit next if
it was up to me
personally i had
a swooning sensation
and when i came
to i was in the
flesh again dad gum
it i lifted first
one leg and then
another to see what i
was this time and
imagine my chagrin and
disappointment when i
found myself inside
another cockroach the
exact counterpart of the
one you smashed whats
the use of dying if
it dont get you
anywhere i was so
sore i went and
murdered a tumblebug i

[430]

suppose as a cockroach
i was not good enough
to be promoted
and not bad enough to
be set back boss a
thing like that makes a
fellow feel awful humble i
came back to town in
that special delivery letter i
would rather dodge
the thing
they cancel stamps with
all day than walk again
say boss
please thank my friends
for all the kind
words and flowers i
must close in haste there
is a new rat
in your office since i
was here last i
wish you would sprinkle a
little cereal in the
bottom of the waste paper
basket

                                    archy

a discussion

there is a good deal
of metaphysical discussion going on
amongst my own little group here
i said freddy the rat was no
more he expired at the moment he
slew that tarantula well he had
once been a human and had
transmigrated into a rat just
as i had transmigrated into a
cockroach the question now
is where will freddy turn up next will
he go up or down the scale and
that has led to the further question as
to what is up and what is down
producing considerable dissension all the
spiders claim they are higher in
the scale than the cockroaches and that
lazy cat mehitabel looks on superciliously
as if confident that she has it on
all of us spiritually speaking
well all i have to say is that in
my case a soul got out of a vers libre
bard into a cockroach but i have
known cases which are exactly the
reverse if you get what i mean
not that i would name any names

archy

quarantined

well boss i suppose you
wonder what has become of
me lately i have been
quarantined or rather
i quarantined myself
voluntarily lest
i help spread the
influenza on the
back of a cockroach
no larger than
myself millions of
influenza germs may lodge i
have a sense of responsibility
to the public and i
have been lying for two weeks
in a barrel of moth
balls in a drug store
without food or water it
strikes me as a good time to
come across with that
raise of salary you
are always promising me
                          archy

archy s statue

say boss but its great to
be famous when i saw that pedestrian
statue of myself on your desk i reflected that not
every one is privileged to see his
monument erected before he dies nor
after either for that matter it
gave me the feeling that i was looking at my own

[433]

tombstone erected in memory of my good
deeds how noble i will have to be to live up
to all that i felt just as a person might
feel who was hearing his own funeral
sermon preached over him i
stared at the statue and the statue stared at
me and i resolved in the future to be
a better cockroach of course it doesn't flatter me
any my middle set of legs arent really
that bowed but the intellectual look
on my face is all there

                                                    archy

the open spaces

one trouble with
cockroaches is that they
do not get
out into the open
air enough
even the tumble
bugs play golf
and it keeps
them serene and
wholesome even the
angle worms feel
drawn to the
brook side in the
spring i am trying
to start a
back to nature movement
among my fellow
cockroaches maybe i
can count on the
co operation of the
housewives league i
am convinced that a
great deal of the

popular prejudice against
cockroaches would
vanish if they
took to the great
open spaces yours
                    archy

short course in natural history

you should be glad
you re not a tomcat
for when all is said
and done
you know youd hate
to pay insurance
on nine lives instead of one
be glad you re not
a centipede
you might your whole
ambition lose
if you had to find
the cash
to keep a centipede
in shoes
be glad you re not
a devilfish
if you had four pairs
of feet
what a trail
you d leave behind you
when you staggered
with the heat
                    archy

[435]

archy protests

well boss now youve got
your desk all cleaned up for the
first time since ive known you what
am i going to do for
a safe retreat in times of dire
need formerly i could crawl under a
bushel of poems and mehitabel the
cat could not find me this
room is as bare as the inside of
a drum you might at
least have left me a tobacco can i
feel as visible as a hyphen and not
half so sure of myself

                     archy

archy on amateur gardens

well boss i have
been looking over your
garden and my
thoughts on the
subject have fallen naturally
into the form of a little
dialogue among the
plants and inhabitants of the
garden to wit as follows

garter snake
how wan on the first of july
the gardens of april appear
now the plants that aspired to the sky
droop and think of the bier

first onion
i am a disillusioned onion plant
so sad so sad am i
that if one fed me to a maiden ant
she would curl up and die

indeterminate vegetable
in youth i hoped a bean to grow
but what i am i do not know

first beet
i have malaria croup and botts

second beet
i have such leprous looking spots

third beet
i was a beet of promise as a young beet
but now i have the mournful feeling
that neither root nor top nor peeling
will ever be fit to eat

garter snake
ah what a melancholy patch

toad
yon egg plant there will never hatch

indeterminate vegetable
one paused by me but yesterday
and spoke of me as hay
but what i really am i do not know

cucumber vine
strange insects walk me to and fro

pepper plant
had i been treated with formaldehyde
that goat that in the dewy eves
came here to feast upon my leaves
might not have died

second onion
the great splay feet of destiny
have trodden me have trampled me

rhubarb
ah once i hoped to line a pie

cucumber vine
will you marauding hen pass by
or must i die

indeterminate vegetable
what thing i am i do not know
men have no name for me

garter snake
i think you are a spinach vine

toad
and i should call you eglantine

sparrow
perhaps you are a pea

first bean
i was a bean
unto some glad tureen
i might have given tone
but a dog yestereen
hiding a bone
took from me all my mundane hope

indeterminate vegetable
sometimes i think i am a canteloupe

second bean
drooping between two hills of corn
i am the butt of all mens scorn

third bean
ah how i aspired
in the glad may morn

fourth bean
i am so tired so tired

sparrow
friend toad from yonder plant keep you away
i saw a neighbor child but yesterday
from off its foliage pluck a spray
and then how he yelled
and his hand turned black and swelled

indeterminate vegetable
perhaps im not a plant at all
but some strange sort of animal

first cabbage
pigeons have riddled me and weasels

second cabbage
im spotted as with german measles

first corn stalk
woe

second corn stalk
woe

third corn stalk
woe is me ah woe woe woe

fourth corn stalk
even the weeds beside me do not grow

first turnip
gott

second turnip
gott gott gott

third turnip
mildew blight and rot

fourth turnip
and smallpox like as not

indeterminate vegetable
but cheer brothers cheer
perhaps before the year
dwindles to winter drear
well poison some one here
i know not what i am
parsley from siam
a vegetable ham
or a long island clam
but this i know i hate
my miserable state
and all human beans
i hate life and fate
i hate men and greens
i hate hens and grass
i hate garden sass
who gets me on a plate
shall learn how i hate
i hate chards romaine
children and goats
old men and young men
people and oats
and im full of ptomaine
who puts me within him
scorpions had better skin him
who puts me inside her
had better eat a spider
i know not what i be
alfalfa corn or pea
but cheer brothers cheer
before the glad new year
well poison some one here

i might give you some advice
about your garden

boss but likely you would
not thank me for it
so i will only make one
suggestion to wit if the
garden were mine i
would set out another cabbage
plant in it and then
give it to the butterflies for
an aviation ground

                    archy

i would rather far get pally with
a pretzel and a seidel

archy on this and that

I

an old stomach
reforms more whiskey drinkers
than a new resolve
and the sexton
stops more than either

2

the world would take its ethics
as seriously as its amusements

three em dash
if they were as amusing

3

a man who is so dull
that he can learn only by personal experience
is too dull to learn
anything important by experience

4

a great many people
who spend their time mourning
over the brevity of life
could make it seem longer
if they did a little more work

5

judging by the number and variety
of pills and religions in the world
the chief preoccupation of man
has been the state of his digestion
and the condition of his soul
and just look at both of them

6

a lot of people
would get back to work now
but they cant afford to take the time off
from keeping the relief agencies going
for if they shut up
that would throw a lot of specialists
out of jobs
i heard one of these bozos
talking to a buddy the other day and made
a little song out of his sentiments
as follows
the dignity of labor
is a phrase i like to see

[443]

imposing on my neighbor
but it cant impose on me
i had rather dilly dally
rest and loaf and idle
i would rather far get pally
with a pretzel and a seidel
of beer

mehitabel sees it through

dear boss i met mehitabel
last night and asked her if
she did not think times were getting
a little better
she was digging for sustenance in a trash heap
at the moment and she looked as if
she might be a part of the heap herself
one of her legs has been damaged again
in a fight with a rival in love
but she began to caper when i spoke to her
and replied as follows

good times and bad times
recoveries and depressions
wotthehell do i care
as long as somethings doing
when i lived on salmon
and oysters stewed in cream
i wasnt always happy
when i dug my scoffins
out of frozen garbage heaps
i wasnt always sad
economic problems
never tell the story
as far as im concerned
once i lived a fortnight
on moonlight wind and grass
and i danced every evening
with the shadows in the alley
and entertained my boy friends
with my melodious songs
wotthehell do i care
if the stomachs empty
when the spirits full
i have had my ups

boss i think mehitabel is mistaken
about the milky way

and i have had my downs
but whether i was up
or whether i was down
there was something in my blood
that always set it dancing
and when the blood was jigging
the feet began to caper
some day i will voyage
on top a garbage scow
just a stiff dead feline
wreathed in orange peel and melon rinds
with shop worn salad garnished
down the bay theyll take me

[446]

to the dumping grounds
defunct as ancient nut shells
but wotthehell do i care
that day has not arrived
and good times or bad times
hard times or easy
there are three good feet
on old mehitabel
and she will keep them jigging
till the grim reaper slices
two more of them off
and then she ll dance on one
till its frozen and resigns
and then her soul will caper
along the milky way
theres a dance or two in the old dame yet
and the word is toujours gai
boss i think mehitabel is mistaken
about the milky way
i think she is more like to dance
on hot cinders in the hereafter
                                archy

mehitabel meets her mate

tis the right of a modern tabby to choose
the cats who shall father her kits
and its nice to be sure their pasts have been pure
and theyre free from fleas or fits

trial marriage i tried till i thoroughly tired
and i suffered somewhat from abduction
and my heart it was broken again and again
but twas excellent instruction

i always have been rather awesomely blest
with the instincts of a mother
and my life and my fate have been down to date
one kitten after another

triplets quadruplets quintuplets
in a most confusing succession
and it seems to keep up whether times are good
or wallowing in depression

and this is in spite of the terrible fact
i am not a real home body
but an artiste who views the domestic career
as damnably dull and shoddy

for i am a lady who has her whims
no tom cat holds my love
if i come to feel i have plighted my troth
to a little mauve turtle dove

but at last i have found my real romance
through the process of trial and error
and he is a ribald brute named bill
one eyed and a holy terror

his skull is ditched from a hundred fights
and he has little hair on his tail
but the son of a gun of a brindled hun
is indubitably male

over the fences we frolic and prance
under the blood red moon
and sing to the stars we are venus and mars
as we caper and clutch and croon

his good eye gleams like a coal of hell
from the murk of alley or yard
and the heart that jumps in the cage of his ribs
is hot and black and hard

says he as we rocket over the roofs
can you follow your limber bill
says i to him my demon slim
theres a dance in the old dame still

you pussies that purr on a persian rug
or mew to some fool for cream
little you know of the wild delight
of the outlaws midnight dream

a fish head filched from a garbage can
or a milk bottle raided at dawn
is better than safety and slavery
you punks that cuddle and fawn

you can stuff your bellies with oysters and shrimp
you may have your ribbon and bell
for bill and me it is liberty
o wotthehell bill wotthehell

says he to me old battle axe
you never was raised a pet
says i to willie i aint any lily
but theres pep in the old dame yet

last night when a bull pup gave us chase
bill turned and a rip of his claw
completely unseamed that slavering mutt
from his chin to his bloody jaw

we dance with the breeze of the summer nights
we dance with the winter sleet
with velvet paws on the velvet shadows
or whirl with frozen feet

we riot over the roof of the world
mehitabel and bill
you son of a gun of a brindled hun
theres a dance in the old dame still

she flung a party in shinbone alley

mehitabel pulls a party

dear boss mehitabel shows
no evidences of reform
she flung a party in shinbone alley
last night and six of the toughest
tabbies i ever saw were her guests
all seven of them danced on the ash cans
flirting their tails in the moonlight
and chanting as follows

oh wotthell do we care
if we are down and out

theres a dance or two in the old janes yet
so caper and swing about
up and down the alley
through and over the fence
for still we are attractive
to various feline gents
meow meow meow

now then sadie dont talk shady
try and remember you and myrtie
that you was raised a lady
that goes for you too gertie
oh i was chased down broadway
by a tom with a ribbon and bell
i says to him my limber jim
you seem to know me well
says he to me oh can it be
you are mehitabel
oh wotthell girls wotthell
as long as the gents is for us
we still got a job in the chorus
we aint no maltese flappers
we all seen better days
but we got as much it
as an ingenue kit
and it is the art that pays
meow meow meow

arch your back and caper
and kick at the golden moon
mebby some yeggs
who sell butter and eggs
will fling us a party soon
now then gertie dont get dirty
frankie frankie dont get cranky
and call any lowlife names
remember that you and your sister
were once society dames
and me and nance was debutants
before we was abducted

remember pearl that you was a girl
that a college went and instructed
dont chew the fat with no common **cat**
for you still got an honored place
oh climb the fence and caper
and kick the moon in the face

oh mebby we all are busted
oh mebby the winters are chill
but all of us girls seen better days
and we are ladies still
remember nell you was once a swell
you was raised a social pet
be careful sweet and act discreet
you may have come down in the world my **dear**
and you got a cauliflower
onto your ear
but you are a lady yet
meow meow meow

oh wotthell oh wotthell
as i came into the alley
i met a brindle swell
he says to me oh this can be
none but mehitabel
oh willie says i as i passed him by
you know me far too well
then cheerio my deario
prance and pirouette
as long as gents has such intents
theres life in the old world yet
meow meow meow

oh wotthell oh wotthell
i spy you brindle bill
come off the fence you feline gents
theres a dance in the old dame still
meow meow miaow
now then girls no shady jests
here come the gentlemen guests

you try and dance refined
remember you all was ladies born
and still are so inclined
now then sadie dont talk shady
or out you go on your nut
this aint any lousy harlem brawl
this aint any party in webster hall
we gotta recall we are nice girls all
and never was anything but
meow meow meow

                archy

was not a ship at all it was a dive in harlem

mehitabel joins the navy

expenses going up
and income going down
but wotthehell do i care
the sailors are in town

a tom cat off a cruiser
was seeing of the city
says he between his whiskers
hello my pretty kitty

oh i am pure and careful
in manner well instructed
i ve seldom spoke to strangers
and seldom been abducted

so i replied discreetly
aint you the nervy guy
how dare you brace a lady
so innocent and shy

oh look he said our warships
have all their flags unfurled
oh come and join the navy
and we will see the world

but the first place that he took me
was not a ship at all
it was a dive in harlem
where they hailed him admiral

a loud shebeen in harlem
which flowed with song and cheer
and we danced upon the tables
for oysters stewed in beer

the second place he took me
he had been there before
we danced for smelt and fishballs
and they called him commodore

twas down in coney island
they named me puss cafe
as we danced among the bottles
for cream and gin frappe

my room rent keeps a mounting
and credit going down
but wotthehell do i care
the sailors are in town

the next place that we landed
he done a noble deed
he sliced the eye from a fresh wharf cat
who tried to make my speed

avast you swabs and lubbers
when a sailor says ahoy
tis a patriotic duty
to give the navy joy

oh i always am the lady
discreet as well as gay
but the next place that he took me
the devil was to pay

for we seen the icebox open
and tried to raid the loot
and the next we knew we was out in the street
ahead of the barkeep s boot

but wotthehell do i care
i neither whine nor fret
what though my spine is out of line
there s a dance in the old dame yet

i would not desert the navy
nor leave it in the lurch
though each place that he took me
was less and less like a church

and now the fleet is sailing
with all its flags unfurled
and five little kittens with anchor marks
are tagging me round through the alleys and parks
but i have seen the world

oh my maternal instinct
has proved to be my curse
it started when i was an ingenue
and went from bad to worse

but wotthehell do i care
whether its tom or bill
for any sailor off of the fleet
there s a dance in the old dame still

mehitabel the cat

what is a lady

mehitabel has
asseverated that
she is a lady
now to decide a bet
will you please
let her tell us
what constitutes
a lady

she must be
an authority on
the subject or else
you would not
print an account
of her doings which seem
to some of us girls
inconsistent with the
standards of
highly respectable conduct
that prevail in this
midvictorian village of
westport conn
i don t know
how it ever got
a name like that
for there ain t anything
sporty about it except it s name
and only half of that
but us girls
want to be ladies and
live up to our
village ideals in
that respect
so please let
mehitabel tell us

what constitutes a lady
and is it
possible for a lady
to be a cat

give my love
to darling archy
    yours truly
            lady bug

p s
do real ladies
smoke pipes
or drink cocktails
or other alcoholic
beverages
or go joy riding
or have
petting parties
or wear onepiece
bathing costumes
where anybody
can see them
or do they instead
knock their
friends and
neighbors every
chance they get
and take a great
interest in civic
affairs and local
politics and
go around
doing good
and being
gracious to
their inferiors

The answer is yes and no.

[458]

he is not true to me what shall i do

archy denies it

dear sir i view with alarm
and it breaks my heart to see it
that archy is associating
with that hussy mehitabel
you must know that he
is my affinity
and my affianced lover
and now he has been going
around with
that disreputable old cat

and he
is not true
to me
what shall i do
i ask you
i am a nice girl
i live in a lovely rosebush
and when we got married
i thought archy would
live at home with me and mama
i am afraid now i will have to break
my engagement
as well as my heart
and i will burn up my
wedding dress which is
beautiful red with polka dots
my life is wrecked
my happiness blighted
o how could he be so false

                              lady bug

When this serious charge was called to the attention
of Archy he hopped over to the typewriter and bumped
out the following reply:

                  this is the sort of thing
                  that happens to people
                  who get their
                  names in the papers
                  that is all
                  the comment i care
                  to make

                              archy

a farewell

archy
i cant believe
you are the hen hater
you profess
you are too handsome
i saw you
the day you walked down
fifth avenue
heading the roach delegation
you were magnificent
as the sun s rays
glinted off
your bronzed back
and your speech was beautiful
about adequate housing
conditions
and better treatment
for stranger cockroaches
within thy gates
but never mind
i will write no more
yet whenever i hear
your name mentioned
i shall be seized in the grasp
of a great grief
thinking what might have been
if you had only known
how really charming
i am
i have letters
from my first two husbands
to prove it
which i have always
kept
farewell
                    jennie

Archy, touched to the quick by the above epistle—and so ignorant of feminine wiles that he does not know **the** females of all species are most dangerous when **they** appear to retreat—dictated the following reply:

> poor thing i wonder
> if it would not be
> a kindness to
> walk by her house
> and let her just
> look at me
> once more
> poor thing
>   archy

archy still in trouble

> archy
> believe me
> i don t quite
> know how to thank you
> for your generous emotion
> over my unfortunate regard
> but i beg of you
> not to permit this melancholy
> to disturb you unduly
> i shall be strong
> and shall throw myself
> into my work
> inspired by the thoughts
> of my happy children
> for i am a good mother
> not like
> mehitabel
>   jennie

> p s on wednesdays at four
> we have tea and nice cakes

at our house
should you care to come
i can promise you
food
that can be trusted
how welcome
you would be
p s no 2
my ancestors
came over on the may flower

To which Archy dictated the following reply:

say doesnt
she know when
she has
been ignored
        archy

the feline tribe were worshipped
in ancient egypt

not any proof

mehitabel the cat
tells me the feline
tribe were worshipped
in ancient egypt
and for that reason i
should hold her in more
respect
well says i
minerva burst from

the head of jove
with a heluva yell
but that does not prove
that we should
stand in awe
of every case of
mastoiditis
    archy

go to the country and become grasshoppers

statesmanship

i was talking
with an insect the
other day about the
hard times that
cockroaches have to
get a living every
mans hand is against them
and occasionally his
foot meals
are few and far between

why in the world
says this
insect do you not
go to the country and become
grasshoppers if
living in town and being
cockroaches is getting
too difficult for you
i was astonished
at the simplicity of the
solution but as i
thought it over it occurred
to me that
perhaps it sounded more
statesmanlike than it
really was
how i asked him are
cockroaches to become
grasshoppers
that is a mere
detail he said which i
leave to you for
solution i have outlined
the general scheme for your
salvation so do not ask
me to settle the mere
details i trust to you for
that you must do
something for yourself
we philosophers cannot do it all
for you unaided you
must learn self help
but alas i fear that
your inherent stupidity will
balk all efforts
to improve your condition
boss i offer you
this little story
for what it is worth
if you are able to

find in it something
analogous to a number
of easy schemes
for the improvement of the
human race you
may do immense good by
printing it
yours for reform
                    archy

a ragout where i may drop in for a warm
bath and a bite to eat

spring

i get about
a good deal
among the insects
especially when
spring arrives
and yesterday
i heard an
argument between
an early cricket
and a busy bee

the cricket spoke
in part as follows

the harps of spring
are in the air
the blackbird
sings
i do not care
a damn if school
keeps in
or not
the jonquil says
all work is rot
the pollywog
has hours to spare

let us rejoice
and from us tear
in glee
our winter
underwear
and let us
dance
and let us
swat
the harps of spring

considering
the lilies there
how do the wicked
ploughmen dare
to lard
their fields with sweat
and plot
increase of gear
by toil begot
we scorn them
we that dance
and bear
the harps of spring

to which the
little busy bee
retorted hummingly
you bards and birds
make such a din
when april s
heedless days begin
flouting
all honest industry
all providence
and husbandry
from every
flower thatched
wayside inn

though heaven
may forgive your sin
of mockery
yet none may win
earth s pardon
for such levity
you bards
and birds
when winter s
sleets
pierce plume and skin
then comes
the ploughman s turn
to grin
by hearth logs
blazing merrily
and feasting burghers
laugh to see
such piping tune fools
cold and thin
you bards and birds

the argument
is one that
does not touch me

[471]

personally
no matter what
the season
i can always find
a ragout
where i may drop in
for a warm bath
and a bite to eat

                    archy the cockroach

the author s desk

i climbed upon my boss his desk
to type a flaming ballad
and there i found a heap grotesque
of socks and songs and salad

some swedenborgian dope on hell
with modernistic hunches
remnants of plays that would not jell
and old forgotten lunches

a plate once flushed with pride and pie
now chill with pallid verses
a corkless jug of ink hard by
sobbed out its life with curses

six sad bedraggled things lay there
inertly as dead cats
three sexless rhymes that could not pair
and three discouraged spats

the feet of song be tender things
like to the feet of waiters
and need when winter bites and stings
sesquipedalian gaiters

peter the pup sprawled on the heap
disputing all approaches
or growled and grumbled in his sleep
or waked and snapped at roaches

i found a treatise on the soul
which bragged it undefeated
and a bill for thirteen tons of coal
by fate left unreceipted

books on the modern girl s advance
wrapped in a cutey sark
with honi soit qui mal y pense
worked for its laundry mark

mid broken glass the spider slinks
while memories stir and glow
of olden happy far off drinks
and bottles long ago

such is the litter at the root
of song and story rising
or noisome pipe or cast off boot
feeding and fertilizing

as lilies burgeon from the dirt
into the golden day
dud epic and lost undershirt
survive times slow decay

still burrowing far and deep i found
a razor coldly soapy
and at the center of the mound
some most surprising opi

some modest pages chaste and shy
for pocket poke or sporran
written by archy published by
doubleday and doran
          archy the cockroach

what the ants are saying

dear boss i was talking with an ant
the other day
and he handed me a lot of
gossip which ants the world around
are chewing over among themselves

i pass it on to you
in the hope that you may relay it to other
human beings and hurt their feelings with it
no insect likes human beings
and if you think you can see why
the only reason i tolerate you is because
you seem less human to me than most of them
here is what the ants are saying

it wont be long now it wont be long
man is making deserts of the earth
it wont be long now
before man will have used it up
so that nothing but ants
and centipedes and scorpions
can find a living on it
man has oppressed us for a million years
but he goes on steadily
cutting the ground from under
his own feet making deserts deserts deserts

we ants remember
and have it all recorded
in our tribal lore
when gobi was a paradise
swarming with men and rich
in human prosperity
it is a desert now and the home
of scorpions ants and centipedes

what man calls civilization
always results in deserts
man is never on the square
he uses up the fat and greenery of the earth
each generation wastes a little more
of the future with greed and lust for riches

north africa was once a garden spot
and then came carthage and rome
and despoiled the storehouse
and now you have sahara
sahara ants and centipedes

toltecs and aztecs had a mighty
civilization on this continent
but they robbed the soil and wasted nature
and now you have deserts scorpions ants and centipedes
and the deserts of the near east
followed egypt and babylon and assyria
and persia and rome and the turk
the ant is the inheritor of tamerlane
and the scorpion succeeds the caesars

america was once a paradise
of timberland and stream
but it is dying because of the greed
and money lust of a thousand little kings
who slashed the timber all to hell
and would not be controlled
and changed the climate
and stole the rainfall from posterity
and it wont be long now
it wont be long
till everything is desert
from the alleghenies to the rockies
the deserts are coming
the deserts are spreading
the springs and streams are drying up
one day the mississippi itself
will be a bed of sand

ants and scorpions and centipedes
shall inherit the earth

men talk of money and industry
of hard times and recoveries
of finance and economics
but the ants wait and the scorpions wait
for while men talk they are making deserts all the time
getting the world ready for the conquering ant
drought and erosion and desert
because men cannot learn

rainfall passing off in flood and freshet
and carrying good soil with it
because there are no longer forests
to withhold the water in the
billion meticulations of the roots

it wont be long now it won't be long
till earth is barren as the moon
and sapless as a mumbled bone

dear boss i relay this information
without any fear that humanity
will take warning and reform
                                        archy